PILGRIMS TO THE HOLY LAND

The Story of Pilgrimage through the Ages

Endpapers: 19th century engraving of Jerusalem, looking west, across the
Vale of Kidron

Thomas Fuller's 17th century map of biblical Palestine
Overleaf: Aerial view of Acre, ancient port of entry for pilgrims of all faiths

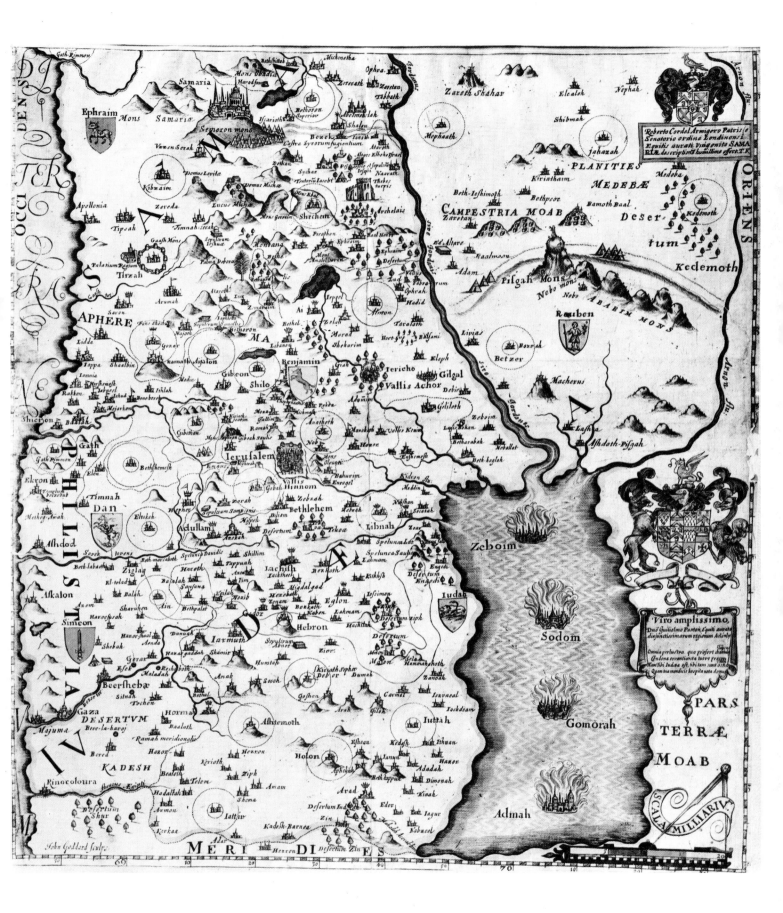

Teddy Kollek and Moshe Pearlman

PILGRIMS TO THE HOLY LAND

The Story of Pilgrimage through the Ages

Harper and Row, Publishers
New York and Evanston

CONTENTS

1 THE ROAD TO JERUSALEM

Israel, land of the Bible, is the oldest country of pilgrimage, and the only one to draw pilgrims of three faiths. Here were enacted the great events recounted in the Old Testament, which are familiar to half the human race, and it was from this soil that there went forth the religious and ethical utterings of the Hebrew prophets which formed the basis of western civilization. It was here that Jesus was born, lived, conducted his Ministry and was crucified, as narrated in the New Testament. And it was here, too, that the followers of Mohammed found sacred associations, believing that it was from a rock in Judea that the prophet made his visionary ascent to heaven.

It is natural, therefore, that Jews and Christians should have been drawn to the scene of the origins of their religions, and Moslems to the site which appeared in a vision to their founder. This country, situated at the eastern end of the Mediterranean at the crossroads of Europe, Asia and Africa, has thus exercised a power of attraction unmatched by any other. It is one of the tiniest countries in the world, but the richest in history. There is hardly a site whose name does not echo down the ages, hardly a mount which does not feature in the biblical record, hardly a spot which does not hold relics of the distant past.

Parts of the timeless landscape look today as they looked when Abraham drove his flocks southward at the beginning of the second millennium BC. The ford across the river Jordan opposite Jericho is much the same as it was when Joshua assembled his people there in the thirteenth century BC. There are environs of Jerusalem which are as they were when king David unified the country and made it the capital in the tenth century BC. One can stride across the very hills of Judea, some still marked by ancient terraces, where Isaiah trod, and Jeremiah, and gaze upon the sights they saw. One can stand today, as Jesus stood, on the Mount of Olives and look down upon the same valley of Kidron – and one can even find shade beneath one of the silvery olive trees in the Garden of Gethsemane where he passed his night of Agony. Along the shores of the Sea of Galilee one can still see the occasional fisherman casting his net with the singular, circular, overhead motion which 'Simon called Peter, and Andrew his brother' must have used when Jesus met them and called upon them to 'follow me, and I will make you fishers of men'. And there are all the other biblical places: Samaria and Joppa (Jaffa), Dan and Beersheba, Endor where Saul took counsel of the witch and Mount Gilboa where he fell in battle, the valley of Elah where David slew Goliath, and the vale of Ajalon where Joshua bade the moon stand still.

To journey back through the centuries, to stand on the very spot where the biblical events took place, to absorb the mood and atmosphere of the past, and also to pay homage at the sacred sites, are what drew pilgrims throughout the ages to these shores. Among them were some who kept careful records of their journeys, the rigours of travel, their adventures en route, and, above all, descriptions of what they saw in the country. It is through the lively, first-hand testimony of the more articulate of these successive pilgrim-reporters that we can today follow the changes from generation to generation in the colour and ambience of this land, and the ideas, customs, legends and patterns of life of the people. These records offer contemporary coverage to each dramatic period in the history of what must assuredly be the most dramatic country in the world.

Jewish pilgrimage began three thousand three hundred years ago with the establishment of the Tabernacle and Ark of the Law at Shiloh by Joshua, afterwards transferred to Jerusalem when king Solomon built the Temple. Christian pilgrimage began some sixteen hundred years later, with the construction of shrines in the fourth century marking the birth and crucifixion of Jesus – three hundred years after those events. Moslem pilgrimage started at the end of the seventh century AD with the building of the Dome of the Rock.

A pilgrimage is a journey undertaken from religious motives to a sacred place, and Christian and Moslem pilgrimage has remained to this day a purely religious undertaking. Jewish pilgrimage began as a religious movement, but later, notably after the destruction of the First Temple and the first exile of the Jewish People from their homeland in the sixth century BC, Jerusalem became the prime symbol of the unity of the Jewish nation, and pilgrimage assumed an additional dimension, taking on a national significance of such magnitude that more than two millennia later, Jewish sovereignty would be regained.

Jewish pilgrimage finds its origin in the biblical injunction contained in Deuteronomy XVI, 16: 'Three times in a year shall all thy males appear before the Lord thy God in the place which he shall choose; in the feast of unleavened bread [Passover, or Pesach], and in the feast of weeks [Pentecost, or Shavuot], and in the feast of tabernacles [Succot].' At first, the specific purpose of the pilgrimage was central worship, and immediately after Joshua's conquest of the country in the thirteenth century BC, 'the whole congregation of the children of Israel assembled together at Shiloh [some twenty miles north of Jerusalem], and set up the tabernacle of the congregation there' (Joshua XVIII, I). Thereafter, throughout the period of the Judges, Shiloh was the place where the Jews gathered in order to worship at festival time, and it gradually became the custom for the whole family, and not only the males, to make the journey.

In the tenth century BC, king Solomon constructed the Temple of the Lord in Jerusalem, and henceforth it was to Jerusalem that the Jews journeyed to celebrate the feasts of Passover, Pentecost and Tabernacles. They thus became known, and are known to this day, as 'The Pilgrim Festivals'.

The site of the Temple was traditionally associated with Mount Moriah, the scene of Abraham's would-be sacrifice of Isaac. This later became the 'threshing floor of Araunah the Jebusite' (II Samuel XXIV) which king David, Solomon's father, had bought for 'fifty shekels of silver'. David had wished to build there a permanent shrine for the Ark of the Law, which in his day was still covered by a nomad's tent, but it had not been given him to do so. This task was undertaken by his son, and on that site, situated on the high ground to the north of the Jerusalem city boundaries as they were in David's day, rose the most spectacular building of the age in the region.

Solomon assembled the finest architects, artists and skilled craftsmen of the day, plus a large army of labourers and porters, and it took them seven years to complete their work. The building was of 'great stones, costly stones, and hewed stones', and the wood used was of 'cedar and fir', acquired from Lebanon under a trade agreement between Solomon and king Hiram of Tyre.

Solomon's Temple was a tall rectangular structure, standing within its own huge court upon what would henceforth be called – to this very day – the Temple Mount. (Modern scholars pin the exact spot to slightly north of where the Dome of the Rock now stands.) Extending from its eastern side was a large porch, and built against the other three walls were 'side chambers'. Inside the Temple was the 'oracle... to set there the ark of the covenant of the Lord', the Ark which had accompanied the Children of Israel from the days of Sinai and which was 'inhabited' by the spirit of the Supreme Being. This 'oracle' was the heart of the Temple, the Holy of Holies, a dark, sombre, gloomy cubicle within the main Temple walls, which contained no image but only the Ark, laid reverently within its inner recesses. And the tone of worship was set on the very first day, the day of its dedication, when 'it came to pass, when the priests were come out of the holy place, that the cloud filled the house of the Lord', and the people of Israel standing outside in the sun-lit court worshipped His presence, while Solomon pronounced the nature of the One God.

Through his words and those of the later Hebrew prophets, the Temple, the Mount and the city of Jerusalem were to be invested with a unique sanctity which the Jewish people were to treasure ever after. They were to remain for all time the fount of the Jewish religion and the focus of the aspirations and yearnings of the

Jewish nation, long after the Temple had been destroyed and throughout all the centuries of the Jewish exile. This yearning, in addition to Jewish pilgrimage, were indeed to be among the prime factors leading to the revival of Jewish statehood in our own day.

With the death of Solomon in 922 BC, the northern tribes revolted and seceded, and the state was thus divided into the northern kingdom of Israel and the southern kingdom of Judah, with Jerusalem, as the political centre, remaining the capital only of Judah. In the initial years of hostility between the two kingdoms, pilgrimage from the northern region virtually ceased. However, since the Temple in Jerusalem symbolized the religious and spiritual centre of the nation, 'the priests and the Levites that were in all Israel... left their suburbs and their possession, and came to Judah and Jerusalem' (II Chronicles XI, 13, 14). This movement helped to sustain Jerusalem through the very difficult years that followed, promoted the subsequent rapprochement between the northern and southern regions, and eventually brought about the restoration of the status, power and influence of Jerusalem over the entire nation, an influence and importance strengthened mightily by the giant Hebrew prophets in the following centuries, notably Isaiah and Jeremiah.

The people of Judah continued throughout the generations to go up to Jerusalem on the three Pilgrim Festivals, and there were frequent appeals to the northerners from the rulers of Judah to do the same, and to suspend political differences at least during the religious occasions. The most powerful entreaty came in the days of king Hezekiah (715-687 BC), who 'sent to all Israel and Judah, and wrote letters also to Ephraim and Manasseh, that they should come to the house of the Lord at Jerusalem, to keep the passover' (II Chronicles XXX, 1), and there is a lively description of how the festival was celebrated. Although the invitation was spurned by many of the tribes, 'Nevertheless some men of Asher and Manasseh and of Zebulun humbled themselves, and came to Jerusalem.' It fell to the great-grandson of Hezekiah, 'the righteous king' Josiah (640-609 BC), to bring the people of the two regions together and to centralize the national worship in Jerusalem. The first festival to be celebrated after he had accomplished this union was Passover, and 'there was no passover like to that kept in Israel from the days of Samuel the prophet; neither did all the kings of Israel keep such a passover as Josiah kept, and the priests, and the Levites, and all Judah and Israel that were present, and the inhabitants of Jerusalem.' (II Chronicles XXXV, 18.) This recognition of the one sanctuary for the One God, the Temple, weakened with the division of the kingdom after Solomon, was now established once and for all. The rulers of the northern territory, to make their political influence more secure, had sought to set up Samaria as a religious rival to Jerusalem. Henceforth, there would be nothing to shake the authority of Jerusalem as Jewry's central shrine and the focus of Jewish pilgrimage.

Top: The biblical injunction to observe the three Pilgrim Festivals, as it appears in a medieval Torah scroll. (Deuteronomy XVI, 16)
Bottom: Baskets of 'first fruits' being brought to the Jerusalem Temple at the Pilgrim Festival of Shavuot. A 19th century engraving

בכל תבואתך ובכל מעשה ידיך והיית אך שמח
שלוש פעמים בשנה יראה כל זכורך את פני
יהוה אלהיך במקום אשר יבחר בחג המצות
ובחג השבעות ובחג הסכות ולא יראה את פני
יהוה ריקם איש כמתנת ידו כברכת יהוה
אלהיך אשר נתן לך שפטים
ושטרים תתן לך בכל שעריך אשר יהוה

16th century Flemish tapestry illustrating the biblical description of king Hezekiah's celebration of the Passover Festival

In the year 587 BC, Jerusalem fell to the Babylonian armies of Nebuchadnezzar and was destroyed. 'They burnt the house of God, and broke down the wall of Jerusalem, and burnt all the palaces thereof with fire, and destroyed all the goodly vessels thereof.' (II Chronicles XXXVI, 19.) Many of the prominent citizens were executed and the rest of the Jews were carried off to exile in Babylon.

By the destruction of their home and the deportation of the survivors, Nebuchadnezzar aimed to bring an end to the Jewish nation. Divorced from their soil and their sanctuary, he thought, they would be swallowed up by the country of their exile and forget their homeland. The effects were quite the reverse. In the hearts of its exiles, Jerusalem continued to live, perhaps occupying a firmer place in their imagination than ever before. It haunted their thoughts and all hopes were centred on its resurrection. The cry they uttered in their immortal lament 'By the rivers of Babylon' re-echoed through all the centuries of Jewish history: 'If I forget thee, O Jerusalem, let my right hand forget her cunning. If I do not remember thee, let my tongue cleave to the roof of my mouth.' (Psalm 137.) The Jews did not forget.

Far from vanishing as a national entity, the Jews in Babylonian exile became a more cohesive community. Away from home, far from their sanctuary, the exiles had perforce to establish local prayer halls – synagogues – in which to worship, and the Pilgrim Festivals could now be celebrated only there, and only with a prayer and a wish – that it would be given to them to resume the pilgrimage 'speedily and in our own days'. This wish, in exile, became at once political as well as religious; for if they were to worship once again at their central shrine, they had to create the political conditions which would make it possible. The religious aim thus became integral to the Jewish national aim for independence.

This aim continued even when the descendants of the deportees began to return to Jerusalem; for they were returning to a city and a country which were still not independent. The first group was enabled to return to build the new Temple – called thereafter the Second Temple – some fifty years later, when Babylon was conquered by Cyrus, founder of a new Persian empire, in the year 539 BC. A ruler with liberal aims towards his subject communities, Cyrus declared himself in favour of the restoration of the Jewish community and religion in their own land, and gave them every help and encouragement. He appointed 'Sheshbazzar, the prince of Judah', governor of the region – which was now a province of Persia – and under him and his successor, Zerubbabel, the Temple was rebuilt. The work was completed in 515.

This was the only construction carried out at that time. Not until several decades later, with the arrival of the large groups of returnees from Babylon under Ezra and Nehemiah in the fifth century BC, were the walls and the city of Jerusalem reconstructed.

The Jews began to rebuild their lives and revive their fields and care for the

Temple according to all the biblical precepts, faithfully following the pilgrimage injunction on the three Pilgrim Festivals. Those beyond Israel's frontiers came to Jerusalem whenever they could, and this practice was increasingly regarded as both a religious and a political act. If they could not come three times a year, they made an annual visit; those who could not manage this tried to come at least once in a lifetime; and those to whom even this was not possible nurtured the hope that it might be. Many unable to do so in life sought to make the pilgrimage in death, instructing that they be buried against the walls of Jerusalem. (There are graves in Jerusalem going back to the second century BC which bear inscriptions of many distant cities in the Near and Middle East from where the bodies had been brought for burial. And in the ancient Jewish cemetery on the Mount of Olives, there are tombstones marking the burial of persons from many parts of the world from early times up to our own day, whose deathbed wish was to be buried in Jerusalem.) The pilgrimage, the hope of pilgrimage even though unfulfilled, and the deathbed wishes kept strong the bond of Jews with Jerusalem.

The Jews in the land of Israel, though not independent, enjoyed a good deal of autonomy in the immediate centuries following their first traumatic experience of exile. Under continued Persian rule there was little discontent and the pilgrimage to Jerusalem was peaceful. In 332 BC, the Persian empire fell before the onslaught of Alexander the Great, the youthful wonder king of Macedonia, which heralded the entry of Hellenism into the Middle East. But Alexander left Jerusalem unharmed, and when he visited the city, he paid his respects with appropriate reverence to the home of Jewry's shrine. In *The Antiquities of the Jews*, Josephus (who was writing four hundred years later, but basing himself on contemporary sources) says that 'Alexander, observing the people... clothed in white, and being preceded by the priests in silken robes, and the high-priest in purple, embroidered with gold, his mitre on his head, and a plate of gold on his forehead inscribed with the sacred name of God, the magnificence of the spectacle struck him with such awe that he advanced alone, and having paid homage to the inscription, saluted the high-priest.'

With the death of Alexander nine years later, control of the country passed to one of his generals, Ptolemy, who proved a ruler of comparative benevolence, as did his successors for more than a hundred years. He exacted tribute from the Jews, but allowed them a considerable measure of self government. They were free to practise their religion and free to continue the pilgrimage.

Incidentally, Ptolemy, who had seized Egypt and made newly established Alexandria his capital, took with him to that country a large number of Jewish prisoners, and from this nucleus there grew the important Jewish community of Alexandria, which soon became the greatest centre of Diaspora Jewry. To them, as to those in other cities in Egypt and elsewhere, Jerusalem remained the city of their devotion and the Temple the centre of their spiritual loyalty. Exile enhanced their feeling of

Aerial view of Jerusalem, from the south. The contours of the hill in right foreground follow the boundary lines of the city in king David's time

fervour towards the Holy City – just as it had that of the Babylonian deportees. When they prayed, they turned to Jerusalem. They were meticulous about their annual Temple tribute. And many made the pilgrimage on one or all of the Pilgrim Festivals.

In 198 BC, the Ptolemies were ousted by the descendants of another of Alexander's generals, Seleucus. At first, the Seleucids were also kindly disposed towards their Jewish community. But with the accession of Antiochus IV Epiphanes in the year 175 there was a drastic reversal of this policy, and he sought to impose upon his Jewish subjects the Hellenistic pattern of life and the worship of Greek gods. It was under Antiochus that the Jews revolted, led by the Hasmoneans (also known as the Maccabees), and in 167 BC they regained their independence. The first act of the Maccabees upon their liberation of Jerusalem was to re-dedicate the Temple, and this act is celebrated by Jews to this day as both a religious and a national holiday. (This is the Festival of Chanuka, or the Feast of Lights.)

The era of complete Jewish independence under the Hasmoneans ended with the Roman conquest in 63 BC by Pompey. Thereafter, even during the periods when the nominal ruler was a Jewish king (but effective power retained by the Romans and the country filled with Roman troops), the population seethed with discontent and rebellion, and the pilgrimage to Jerusalem became a mass demonstration of resistance, at times passive, at times explosive. When foreign rule was particularly tyrannous, the Pilgrim Festivals were often the occasion for open insurrection.

Twenty-three years after Pompey's entry into Jerusalem, the Jews briefly regained their independence under the last of the Hasmoneans, king Mattathias Antigonus. But three years later, in 37 BC, Herod, who had been made king of Judea by the Romans, marched on Jerusalem at the head of a powerful force, including two Roman legions, and captured the city. Thus began an extraordinary reign which ended with his death in 4 BC.

Herod, grandson of an Idumean convert to Judaism, friend of Rome, who ruled his Jewish subjects with a crushing hand, had a passion for building, and remains of his extraordinary structures may be seen today. He built the dramatic fortress on the top of Masada overlooking the Dead Sea, which was recently excavated. He built the remarkable palace-fortress on the peak of Herodium, a few miles from Bethlehem, where he was buried. He created the city of Caesarea on the Mediterranean coast and endowed it with buildings of such opulence that the Romans later used it as their capital. And he was responsible for raising other cities, fortifications and palaces in other parts of the country. He also changed the skyline of Jerusalem, and today's Old City is full of Herodian remains. He built the formidable Antonia Fortress at the northwestern corner of the Temple Mount so that Roman troops could more easily supervise the huge crowds of pilgrims at

Jewish festivals and 'watch for any sign of popular discontent', as Josephus relates. (Parts of this structure may be seen today in the Convent of the Sisters of Zion just inside the Lions' [also called St Stephen's] Gate.) He built his own palace (adjoining today's Jaffa Gate) of stately magnificence and fortified it so heavily that it was really a citadel commanding the Upper City, as it was then known, of Jerusalem. It was subsequently used as the residence of Roman procurators and in the later periods of occupation as a garrison or fortress, and is known to this day as the Citadel. (It is also called The Tower of David, though it has no Davidic associations, and we shall find it referred to by either name when we read the descriptions of the pilgrim-reporters.)

But the most spectacular of all Herod's building projects in Jerusalem was his reconstruction of the Temple. He followed the original biblical ground-plan of the buildings devoted to worship, but he doubled the height of its golden façade and considerably extended its porch. To set it on a suitable base and make it the central feature of the landscape, Herod covered the Temple Mount with a huge rectangular platform, supported by substructures and towering retaining walls. A section of one of these walls is today's 'Western Wall' (called by Christians the 'Wailing Wall'), revered by Jews for the last nineteen hundred years as their most sacred holy place.

Upon the topmost terrace of this Temple esplanade stood the House of Worship, and below it on descending terraces the various courts and auxiliary structures which constituted the Inner Temple, the whole surrounded by a wall and ritual fence. On the terrace below, the floor of the esplanade, and running round the Inner Temple, was the Outer Court, or Court of the Gentiles, enclosed by massive walls and encompassing the entire Temple compound, an area of 140,000 square yards. There were gates in all four sides, but the most remarkable, and of special interest to the modern pilgrim, were the entrances in the west, used by the priests and the royal family. This is the side where the Temple compound was separated from the Upper City by the central valley, later known as the Tyropoeon valley, and to link them Herod built two great bridges, resting on massive arches of stone. The priests' bridge reached the Temple Mount at a point a few yards north of today's Western Wall, and the royal bridge just south of it. Remains of both bridges are now visible to all, through archaeological excavations, but they were hidden to pilgrims throughout the centuries and thus find no mention in their records.

They were mentioned, however, with copious descriptions, in the works of Josephus as well as in the Mishnah, so that they were known to historians. In 1838, the American scholar Edward Robinson, 'father' of biblical geography, on a visit of exploration and survey, detected a ridge of curved stones jutting out of the Western Wall which he identified as the springer to an arch of one of the Herodian bridges. Some thirty years later, the British archaeologist Captain (later General

2nd century BC to 1st century AD ossuaries found in Jewish burial caves
on the Mount of Olives

Sir) Charles Wilson came upon another arch north of Robinson's find which he identified as belonging to the second bridge. The two finds were known thereafter as Robinson's Arch and Wilson's Arch.

Following the 1967 Six Day War, Israel archaeologists headed by Professor Benjamin Mazar of the Hebrew University started a comprehensive excavation of the area. They found part of the base, preserved to a height of 15 feet, of Robinson's Arch, whose span was now seen to be more than 300 feet and whose width was more than 50 feet. On the Wilson site, all the debris was cleared, and what is visible today is one complete arch in a perfect state of preservation, the huge Herodian stones immaculately laid to form a flawless curve. It was opened to the public in 1969 and it looks much as it must have done in Herod's day.

The Mazar expedition also made a discovery directly related to ancient pilgrimage. Their excavations brought to light an extensive Herodian plaza, some forty feet wide, alongside the Western Wall, where worshippers who had come for the Pilgrim Festivals would congregate. After the Temple service, the pilgrims held holiday feasts in the area, and the archaeologists found a considerable quantity of cooking vessels and crockery which had been deliberately broken. The indication is that these vessels were used only once, and for each Pilgrim Festival new vessels would be brought.

The expedition also found, after digging down forty feet below the present level, the large Herodian terrace in front of the double-gate of the southern wall, which was the main entrance to the Temple compound for the general public.

Though the truly pious pilgrim would have been drawn to the place of worship even if it had been no more than a modest tent – as it was at Shiloh – undoubtedly the grandeur of the physical structure of the shrine served as an added attraction to the general populace from the time of Solomon. With Herod's magnificent reconstruction – and improved communications in Roman times – not only Jews but people of other religions, and of no religion, came in increasing numbers to gaze and wonder at the hill-top Jewish Temple in the already renowned city of Jerusalem. The variety of countries from which the pilgrims came, Jews, proselytes and Gentiles, is mentioned by Josephus and in the New Testament, and they range from Asia in the east to Rome in the west.

Incidentally, the most noted proselytes who made the pilgrimage in the first century AD were the royal family of Adiabene, a Mesopotamian principality. On her visit to Jerusalem, the queen mother Helen also erected a lavish family tomb a few hundred yards beyond the northern wall of the city which became known as 'The Tomb of the Kings'. The courtyard and great staircase leading down to the tomb, which still stand, are often referred to in the pilgrim records.

If Jerusalem gave much to the pilgrims, the pilgrims also gave much to Jerusalem. Pilgrimage made and kept Jerusalem a cosmopolitan city from early times. It also

The ornate 1st century AD 'Tomb of the Kings' in Jerusalem, was erected
by the royal family of Adiabene, proselyte pilgrims

brought an expansion to its building. Hostels for the needy were erected by the city authorities and private villas were often put up by the wealthier pilgrims. Some Diaspora communities built and maintained their own synagogues there – in itself an indication of the scale of the pilgrimage – so that when they were not sacrificing in the Temple they could gather in a familiar House of Worship and read and study the Law in the accent and custom of their own congregation.

The major pilgrimage was from Alexandria in Egypt, Antioch in Syria and Babylon in Mesopotamia, the principal Jewish centres of exile; but from inscriptions on antiquities and frequent mention in the Talmud, we know that Jews came from as far as the distant townships on the periphery of the Roman empire.

Organized caravans plied the domestic pilgrimage routes, and overseas visitors joined the local pilgrims. Up-country villagers would assemble at their regional centre, camp out overnight and start off early in the morning. Clans and often entire villages would make the journey together. In 66 AD, when Cestius Gallus, the Roman governor of Syria, was on his way south in his unsuccessful attempt to smother the Jewish outbreak in Jerusalem, he 'marched from Antipatris to Lydda', according to Josephus, but 'he found the city empty... for the whole multitude were gone up to Jerusalem to the feast of the Tabernacles'. The caravans would cover a scheduled distance each day, and the pilgrims, some walking, some riding on donkey or camel, would sing psalms as they approached the golden city. At the gates of the capital, thronged with colourful crowds, stood chanting priests and choirs. Welcoming the pilgrims was a delegation of city elders. Once inside the city, the pilgrims bathed and changed into white robes, and were now ready to visit the Temple.

In the last year of Herod's reign, among the Jewish villagers from Galilee who visited the Temple were a family from Nazareth, Joseph and Mary and their baby son, Jesus. He had been born in Bethlehem a few weeks earlier, his parents having gone there 'to be taxed'. Now, after 'eight days were accomplished for the circumcising of the child... And when the days of her purification according to the law of Moses were accomplished,' before returning to Nazareth, 'they brought him to Jerusalem, to present him to the Lord.' (Luke II, 21, 22.) Thereafter, as infant and child, he was taken by his father and mother on their annual pilgrimage, for 'his parents went to Jerusalem every year at the feast of passover' (Luke II, 41).

In the year 33 AD, Jesus came again to Jerusalem, as was his wont, on the Festival of Passover. It was to be his final pilgrimage. It was then that he was seized by the Romans, brought before Pontius Pilate, judged, condemned, taken off to Golgotha (Calvary) and crucified. Three hundred years later, the sites associated with the birth and final days of this Jewish pilgrim were themselves to become hallowed sites of a new pilgrimage to the followers of a new faith, Christianity.

This faith sprang up and developed far from the scene of Jesus' last ministry,

Top: Entrance to Warren's Shaft (beneath Wilson's Arch) exposing the lower courses of the Herodian wall of the Temple Compound, Jerusalem

Bottom: 19th century engraving of Sir Charles Warren's discovery and excavation of the shaft

Overleaf: Southwest corner of the Temple compound, the site of current archaeological excavations. The walls are Herodian (except for the top courses)

notably in Antioch and other parts of the Middle East and the eastern Mediterranean, where his disciples recounted his teachings, his parables, the stories of his miracles in his lifetime and his Resurrection and Ascension. Jerusalem itself, bristling with rebellion against the regime of Rome, a mood only exacerbated by the frequent Roman crucifixion of 'trouble-makers', remained comparatively untouched by the views expounded by the latest victim of Rome. The Jews adhered to their own religion, and maintained a smouldering resistance to Rome which erupted from time to time into open battle. In 66 AD it exploded into country-wide war, which lasted five years and ended with the destruction of the Temple and Jerusalem by Titus in 70 AD.

Scores of thousands of Jewish fighting men had been killed in battle. Equally large numbers of civilians, the aged, the weak, women, children, and priests were butchered by Roman legionaries on their victory rampage. Many able-bodied survivors were executed, or saved for death in gladiatorial combat, or carried off as slaves. But a number of Jews remained alive in the rest of the country, and when the orgy of killing had subsided, they began to pick up the broken threads of their communal and religious existence, their centre of gravity shifting first to the seat of Talmudic learning at Yavne (near Ashkelon on the Mediterranean coast) and later to Galilee. And they, together with Jews of the Diaspora communities, would make the pilgrimage to a shattered Jerusalem, their mourning over its destruction mingled with the hope of and confidence in its restoration.

There is a Tractate (Makkot, 24b) in the Babylonian Talmud which offers a glimpse into this dark period. It tells of Rabbi Akiba, the greatest Talmudic scholar of his age, accompanied by three companions 'coming up to Jerusalem together', and when they reached Mount Scopus and looked down upon the ruined city, they rent their garments in the traditional gesture of mourning. As they approached the Temple site, they saw a jackal bounding out of the rubble that had been the Holy of Holies. His companions wept. Rabbi Akiba smiled.

'Why do you smile?' they asked.

'Why do you weep?' said he.

'We see the ruins of our Holy Sanctuary, that is now become the haunt of jackals, and should we not weep?'

Said Rabbi Akiba: 'Therefore do I smile. The Prophets foretold both the destruction of Jerusalem and its restoration to glory. Now I have seen the first prophecy come to pass, and I know that the second will also be fulfilled.'

His companions said: 'Akiba, thou hast comforted us.'

Rabbi Akiba did more than give comfort. He put his spiritual weight behind the renewal of Jewish resistance which had begun to develop not long after Jerusalem had fallen. When the heroic figure of Bar Kochba emerged, Akiba the Sage joined him in a powerful call to arms, and the Jews rose and fought their last desperate War of Freedom against the Romans. The rising was touched off by the

Model of the Temple compound at the time of the Second Temple, with Herod's Antonia Fortress at northwest corner. The model is in the grounds of the Holyland Hotel, Jerusalem

action of emperor Hadrian who had issued a series of decrees aimed at wiping out all trace of Judaism and Jews from their Holy City. Bar Kochba scored an initial success. Jewish independence was regained and Jerusalem restored as capital and religious centre. This lasted three years, from 132 to 135 AD. Hadrian then brought in a great army and after grim fighting, Roman rule was re-established. (Akiba died under torture by his captors.)

Hadrian could now carry out his original aim. He razed Jerusalem and upon its ruins erected a new city which he renamed Aelia Capitolina. (Aelius was Hadrian's family name and Capitoline Jupiter was the principal Roman god.) There was to be no trace of its former Jewish associations, and upon the site of the Temple he built a temple to Jupiter, with an equestrian statue of himself in front of it. An edict went out forbidding any Jew to enter the city, or even come within sight of it, with the death penalty for transgressors. This prohibition was to remain in force up to the fourth century AD, when it was slightly eased, Jewish pilgrims being permitted to visit the Temple site once a year, on the ninth of the Jewish month of Av, anniversary of the destruction of their central shrine. In the fifth century AD, the ban was lifted completely and Jews were allowed once again to settle in the city.

There is surely deep significance in the fact that for the two hundred years that Jerusalem was the pagan town called Aelia Capitolina, bereft of a Jewish community and barred to Jewish pilgrims, this history-laden and history-making city seems to have dropped out of the mainstream of history, playing no major part in the life of the country. It was still a handsome town, with lavish buildings constructed by Hadrian, but the life that proceeded within its new walls was that of a dull, unimportant, provincial settlement.

The Roman centre of this territory was Caesarea, the city on the Mediterranean coast which Herod had built at the end of the first century BC as a monument to his royal Roman patron, Caesar Augustus, after whom it was named. He built a deep water harbour and a town of majestic size, as we know from the archaeological remains and from the eye-witness report of Josephus. It was from this city, not from Jerusalem, that the Romans governed their province of Syria Palaestina. Caesarea, as we shall see, was to figure in the pilgrim reports of later centuries.

During this period, with their sacred capital denied to them, the decimated Jewish community made Galilee their physical centre, establishing there the Sanhedrin, schools of study and synagogues. Yet from Talmudic sources we know that in the third century there were individual Jews who braved the death penalty and made the pilgrimage to the Temple site.

Yemenite Jews mourn the destruction of the Temple at the Western Wall on the anniversary fast-day, 9th of the Hebrew month of Av

CONSTANTINVS AVG

2 CONSTANTINE AND HELENA

The two individuals who did more than anyone to make Palestine a centre of Christian pilgrimage – and also to ensure the spread of Christianity – were Constantine the Great and his mother, queen Helena, both converts from paganism. Constantine was the first Roman emperor to adopt Christianity and he raised it from a system of faith followed by a minority of scattered groups to the official religion of his empire. By this act, he secured its future.

Constantine had started his rule in the year 306 AD as the junior caesar governing the western parts of the empire. By 324, he emerged as the sole Roman ruler over all the dominions, east and west, with the title of emperor, and he retained sole power until his death in 337. His capital was Byzantium (which he rebuilt and renamed Constantinople in 330 – though Byzantium was the name given to the eastern empire when the Roman empire was divided later in the century), and Palestine now came under his direct rule.

By the time he reached the imperial throne, Constantine had become deeply involved with the new religion, and in the year 325 he convened the first ecumenical council of the Christian Church at Nicaea (near Byzantium) which was attended by prelates from all his territories. Of high importance was the formulation of dogma at this convocation; but perhaps more so was the presence there of queen Helena, who had accompanied her son; for there she met the delegate from the city still called Aelia Capitolina, Bishop Macarius. He reported to her that nothing had been done since the Crucifixion to commemorate and preserve the sites where the dramatic events of the last hours of Jesus had been enacted. To do so now, he urged, was surely the greatest act for the furtherance of the new faith that the emperor could perform. Queen Helena was greatly moved by this appeal and so was her son when she told him. A year later, in 326 AD, she journeyed to Jerusalem – the name Aelia was subsequently abandoned – and together with Macarius determined the locations where Jesus had been crucified and buried. They decided that the two sites were close to each other, and over them Constantine caused to be erected a great shrine, the Church of the Holy Sepulchre, which became the most sacred shrine in Christendom and the focus of Christian pilgrimage.

Constantine the Great. A sculpture at San Giovanni in Laterano, Rome

33

Now that the Temple lay in ruins, the new church was the most imposing structure in the city, and indeed, no expense had been spared. In a letter to Macarius commissioning the building, Constantine had written: 'It is fitting that your sagacity do so order and make provision for everything necessary, that not only shall this basilica be the finest in the world, but that the details also shall be such that all the fairest structures in every city may be surpassed by it...'

'These things did the emperor write, and his instructions were at once carried into effect,' says Eusebius (260-340), ecclesiastical historian, bishop of Caesarea and one of the great figures of the early church. Eusebius saw the shrine being built and was present at its consecration in 335, and he called it 'a spectacle of surpassing beauty'.

Its dominant feature was the great rotunda of the Anastasis (site of the Resurrection), in the centre of which lay the sepulchre, encircled by columns and topped by a huge dome. Adjoining this circular shrine was a cloistered open court which contained the rock of Golgotha. Leading off this court was a rectangular basilica, the Martyrium, with two rows of pillars on either side of the nave, the apse placed, unusually, at the western end so that it lay in the direction of the sepulchre. Adjoining the other end, giving entrance to the basilica, was the atrium, a covered portico.

[The Church of the Holy Sepulchre underwent several repairs and restorations in the centuries that followed without much change in its architectural form. The Crusaders, however, carried out a radical reconstruction, completed in 1149, incorporating all the buildings and court under a single roof, with the rotunda still the principal feature, and this remains the broad plan of the Church today, though there are of course sundry additions since Crusader times, such as the marble enclosure to the sepulchre, the marble covering to the rock of Calvary, a bell-tower, the Stone of Anointing, and several chapels and oratories.]

From Jerusalem, queen Helena and Bishop Macarius went to Bethlehem, four miles away, and there determined the grotto where Jesus was born. Constantine erected there the Church of the Nativity, consisting of an octagonal structure above the grotto – one of several caves on the site – and adjoining it, a basilica divided into nave and twin aisles by rows of monolithic columns, and richly decorated with marble, mosaics and frescoes. An opening was cut in the rock roof of the grotto so that visitors entering the octagonal sanctuary could glimpse the traditional birth-place and manger below.

[The church was badly damaged two hundred years later and completely rebuilt by the Byzantine emperor Justinian I in the middle of the sixth century. The octagonal structure gave way to an enlarged chancel above the grotto, and the grotto could be reached – as it can be today – by two stairways running down to it on either side of the chancel. The basilica was extended and a portico added. The columns were re-set. A new floor was laid above the debris which covered the

The Greek Orthodox Chapel of Calvary in the Church of the Holy Sepulchre, Jerusalem

original Constantinian mosaic. (Part of this mosaic may be seen today through an opening in the floor of the nave.) With all the subsequent repairs and restorations, today's Church of the Nativity is basically Justinian, though instead of the three doors of the original façade, there is now a low entrance-way which was specially made at the beginning of the sixteenth century to prevent marauders on horseback from desecrating the church. Above this entry may still be seen the pointed arch of the Crusader entrance, and above it is part of the cornice of Justinian's central door. The stairways from the chancel to the grotto meet before the Altar of the Nativity where a star set in white marble marks the site of the birth. Nearby is the site of the manger.]

As a Christian holy place and as a site of pilgrimage, Constantine's Church of the Nativity was, and is, second only to the Church of the Holy Sepulchre. Almost as soon as they were erected, both immediately drew pilgrims from afar, quite a number of whom stayed. Among them were many who came to live out their lives as monks or nuns close to these sites. To provide accommodation and prayer halls for the growing Christian community and overseas pilgrims, wealthy Christians followed the Constantine example and built monasteries, convents, hospices, churches and chapels in and around Jerusalem and Bethlehem and also in the Judean desert, which had begun to attract hermits as a place of retreat and meditation. These in turn drew even more pilgrims and added greater variety and interest to their pilgrimage.

In the north, too, there were places to visit — Nazareth, where Jesus spent his boyhood; the banks of the Sea of Galilee where he met the fishermen; Cana, where he performed his first miracle of water into wine; and all the other places mentioned in the New Testament. Soon, each of these sites would be commemorated by a church or a monastery, which in turn would find its place in the itinerary of later pilgrims.

There has been much scholarly controversy over the authenticity of a number of sites venerated by pilgrims. Some are quite definitely authentic and arouse no argument, their identification being based either on tangible relics or detailed records, or both. Into this category fall, for example, Jerusalem's Temple compound and the Western (Wailing) Wall, the spring of Gihon and Pool of Siloam and king Hezekiah's water tunnel. Then there are sites like Antonia Fortress, which certainly existed and whose tangible remains may be seen today; but whereas tradition holds this to be the place where the trial of Jesus was conducted, some modern scholars argue (and at least one fourth century pilgrim wrote) that Pilate held the trial in what had formerly been Herod's palace (today's Citadel). Finally, there are lesser sites with a weaker tradition which may have developed through an encounter by a persuasive local inhabitant with an overly gullible early pilgrim.

However, what is perhaps of supreme importance, and assuredly what was in the minds of all pilgrims and visitors, ancient and modern, is that the whole country is *authentic* – this is where it all happened! Not every site in the Bible has been the subject of, and confirmed by, an archaeological excavation, like the 'chariot cities' built by king Solomon which were unearthed in this century. But if you move through the length and breadth of this land, you may be certain of striking a path trodden by king David and Isaiah and Amos and Nehemiah and Judah the Maccabee and Jesus and view the same landscapes they witnessed. It is this kind of experience, to be on the same soil and under the same patch of sky as the biblical characters, which drew, and draws, the pilgrim to this land – though certainly the shrines, sanctuaries and commemorative monuments exercise a formidable, additional attractive power.

The earliest record of a Christian pilgrim which has come down to us is that of a Gaul from Bordeaux who described his journey to the Holy Land in the year 333 AD. The report of his travels is set forth in his *Itinerary from Bordeaux to Jerusalem* which he evidently compiled for the use of his countrymen.

With the comparative tranquillity and security which Constantine brought to his empire, our pilgrim set out with favourable prospects of reaching his goal. From Gaul, he crossed the Alps into Italy, passed through Turin, Pavia, Milan, Verona, crossed the Julian Alps, went into Thrace and on to Byzantium (newly renamed Constantinople), and thence, after crossing the Bosphorus, he continued through Asia Minor to Syria, and reached Palestine at Acco. He covered, on his reckoning, 3,250 miles, stopping over at 190 stations and changing horses no less than 360 times.

From northern Palestine he travelled down the coast to Caesarea, where there 'is the bath of Cornelius the centurion' who had been baptized by Peter, and from there, to Jerusalem via Samaria, visiting Old Testament sites like Shechem (today's Nablus) and giving their biblical history. His description of Jerusalem suggests that it followed the same plan as Aelia Capitolina; but Hadrian's pagan temples had now been torn down, and where the shrine to Venus had stood, there now rose Constantine's basilica, 'a church of wondrous beauty'. On the site of the Temple, our pilgrim saw a 'stone, to which the Jews come every year and anoint it, bewail themselves with groans, rend their garments, and so depart'. Thus, by the time of his visit, the rigidity of Hadrian's ban on Jews had been relaxed by Constantine to permit them a one-day-a-year pilgrimage of mourning.

The Christian community grew and the building of shrines and hospices in Jerusalem continued apace under Constantine and his son. But in 361 AD the man who succeeded to the imperial throne was Constantine's nephew, emperor Julian, known ever after as 'The Apostate' because he publicly disavowed the Christian faith, struggled determinedly against it, and issued an edict of universal toleration.

A mother-of-pearl model of the Church of the Holy Sepulchre on display in the Museum of the Flagellation, Jerusalem

Julian authorized the restoration of the Jewish Temple, and all the preparatory work of construction was put in hand; but actual building had hardly begun before Julian was mortally wounded (363 AD) in his ill-fated campaign against the Persians. His successor as emperor was as Christian as his predecessor, and the Temple project was cancelled.

However, during Julian's three-year reign, Jerusalem was again open to Jewish pilgrims, and not only on the annual day of mourning. An extraordinary recent archaeological discovery echoes the joy that was felt by the Jews at that time. In May 1969, in the course of his excavations at the southwest corner of the Temple compound, Professor Benjamin Mazar discovered a Hebrew inscription in the sixth course of the Herodian wall below the springer of Robinson's Arch, the archaeological stratum belonging to the middle of the fourth century AD, the time of Julian. The beautiful Hebrew lettering was the work of a skilled craftsman and was executed at the behest of Jewish pilgrims. It is part of verse 14 of Isaiah, chapter 66, coming just after 'ye shall be comforted in Jerusalem', and it reads: 'And when ye see this, your heart shall rejoice, and your bones shall flourish like an herb.'

וראיתם ושש לבכם
ועצמותיכ כדשא

After the Gaul from Bordeaux, the next literary pilgrim whose record has come down to us was also French. This was (St) Silviae, a lady from Aquitania (near the Rhone valley) who made the journey in about the year 385. She must have been a most formidable personage to undertake such extensive and arduous travels, lasting several years, through the heat and dust of the Middle East, visiting every holy place she could think of.

Some scholars have questioned the authorship of *The Pilgrimage of St Silviae*, holding that Silviae was a known ascetic of a very severe type, whereas, as one scholar says, 'there is no trace of asceticism in the conduct or language' of the author of this document. She grumbles much over the steepness of Mount Sinai, and seems to regret that she cannot be carried up in a chair. To support his thesis, this scholar quotes from another document known to have been written by St Silviae which incidentally throws light on the habits of the more self-mortifying of the pilgrims. She wrote: 'I am now more than sixty years of age; but except the tips of my

Byzantine statue in marble of 'The Good Shepherd', found in the ruins
of an ancient church at Al-Mina, near Gaza

fingers (and that for the purpose of communicating) no water has ever touched my face, or my feet, or any of my limbs. Even when, being seized with various diseases, I was urged by the physicians to take a bath, I could not endure to give the flesh its due. I have never slept on a couch or travelled anywhere in a litter.'

Our pilgrim, whoever she was, made Jerusalem her base and journeyed out from there, proceeding first to the wild and forbidding country in the southern Sinai Peninsula with its rugged cluster of gaunt peaks. One of them, according to early Christian tradition, was Mount Sinai or Mount Moses, where the Ten Commandments were received (though most modern scholars dispute the theory that the Exodus route took the Children of Israel past this mount). However, the belief was held strongly enough in those days to have attracted monks and hermits to this site, and Constantine had erected a chapel on what was held to have been the place of the Burning Bush at the foot of a lower slope nearby, together with a refuge tower for the hermits. (In the sixth century, emperor Justinian I added an entire monastery complex and enclosed the whole with a high wall of grey granite. Several centuries later it became known as St Catherine's Monastery, and today's structure is basically the fortress-like building of Justinian.)

Our pilgrim returned to Jerusalem, and there is one feature of special interest in her account of the Holy Sepulchre services on Good Friday, which shows that by the time of her visit the True Cross seems to have been 'discovered' – though there is no mention as yet of the attribution of the 'discovery' to queen Helena, as was made in later pilgrim records. Silviae related a strange incident while describing the Good Friday ritual of exhibiting the cross: 'A chair is placed for the bishop in Golgotha... [when he] sits down in the chair, there is placed before him a table covered with a linen cloth, the deacons standing round the table. Then is brought a silver-gilt casket, in which is the holy wood of the cross; it is opened, and the contents being taken out, the wood of the cross and also its inscription are placed on the table. When they have been put there, the bishop, as he sits, takes hold of the extremities of the holy wood with his hand, and the deacons, standing round, guard it. It is thus guarded because the custom is that every one of the people... leaning forward, bend over the table, kiss the holy wood, and pass on. And as it is said that one time a person fixed his teeth in it, and so stole a piece of the holy wood, it is now guarded by the deacons standing round, so that no one who comes may dare to do such a thing again.'

It was another pilgrim of the period, also a lady, who recorded these pastoral impressions as she moved through Judea and approached Jerusalem: 'In the village of Christ, all is rusticity, and, except for psalms, silence. Whithersoever you turn, the ploughman holding the plough-handle sings Alleluyah; the perspiring reaper diverts himself with psalms, and the vine-dresser sings the Songs of David while he trims the vine with his curved knife. These are the ballads of this country, these

St Catherine's Monastery in Sinai
Overleaf: Scenes from 'Legend of the True Cross', celebrated 15th century fresco by Piero Della Francesca, in the Church of S. Francesco, Arezzo

are the love-songs, as they are commonly called. These are whistled by the shepherds and are the implements of the husbandman.'

The writer was a matron of Rome named (St) Paula, of ancient lineage, great wealth and high social rank, urging her friend Marcella to undertake the pilgrimage. It was at Marcella's house that she had met and come under the influence of (St) Jerome, the most erudite churchman of his time, who was then serving as secretary to the Pope. Together with her daughter Eustochium, Paula left Rome in the spring of 382, and on her journeys to the sacred sites in the Holy Land, she was accompanied for much of the time by Jerome. It was he who wrote the account of her experiences in his *The Pilgrimage of the Holy Paula*. (The letter to Marcella, however, is in her own words.)

Paula's first reaction to cosmopolitan Jerusalem is disappointing. It is too 'worldly'. But then she hastened to the Church of the Holy Sepulchre, where, as Jerome writes, 'prostrate before the cross, she adored it as though she saw the Lord hanging upon it'. In Bethlehem, 'entering the Grotto of the Saviour, when she saw the holy inn of the Virgin and the stable... she declared that, by the eyes of faith, she could see the Infant Lord, wrapped in swaddling-clothes, wailing in the manger, the Magi adoring, the star shining above... the shepherds coming by night...'

Bethlehem was the place which had moved her most, and when Jerome settled there, Paula decided to do so too, 'building cells and monasteries, and founded inns for different kinds of pilgrims by the side of the road upon which Mary and Joseph found no resting place'. She died in the year 404, Jerome some sixteen years later, having written his major ecclesiastical works in Bethlehem and produced the Vulgate, his Latin translation from the original Hebrew of the Old Testament. (After his death, Bethlehem sites associated with him became subsidiary targets of pilgrimage, and remain so to this day. The grotto beneath the Church of the Nativity gives access to other caves, one of which is called the Chapel of St Jerome and is said to have been the cell where he dwelt and wrote. A nearby cave is held to have been his tomb.)

The period from the middle of the fifth to the middle of the sixth century AD was the peak period of Christian 'discovery', with the finding of relics associated with Jesus, his family, disciples and friends which started cherished traditions. The last pilgrim tract to have come down to us which was written, as the 19th century British explorer General Sir Charles Wilson has pointed out, 'before it had become the fashion to stimulate the devotion of pilgrims by the exhibition of relics connected with our Lord's Passion' was *The Epitome* of Bishop Eucherius of Lyons in about 440 AD. This report mentions no relics. The change that took place in the next century is well seen by comparing this tract with *The Breviary*, written by an unknown pilgrim in about the year 530 as a guide to prospective pilgrims. By now, not only had the True Cross been found – as was mentioned by St

Star marking the site of the Nativity in the Grotto of the Church of the Nativity in Bethlehem

Silviae – but 'as one enters the church of the Holy Constantine, there is a large apse on the western side, wherein the three crosses were found', namely the cross upon which Jesus was crucified and the ones for the two thieves crucified with him. The tradition also developed that the True Cross had been found by empress Helena, with the thought, no doubt, that attribution to the mother of Constantine would carry greater credibility. (Scholars point out that so important a discovery would assuredly have been noted by Eusebius – a contemporary of Helena – in the description he wrote of the shrine just after its consecration in his *Life of Constantine*.) At all events, a disused cistern beneath the church became, and is still called, the Crypt or Chapel of the Finding of the Cross, and just above it is another crypt which is called the Chapel of St Helena.

The writer of *The Breviary* then listed other relics which are now on display. He directs us to a chamber in the Holy Sepulchre compound 'in which is the reed, and the sponge, and also the cup which the Lord blessed and gave to His disciples to drink, saying "This is My body and My blood".' Elsewhere in the compound 'stands that basilica in which is the spear with which our Lord was pierced'. He mentions the church on Mount Zion 'wherein is the column at which the Lord Jesus was scourged. One may see the print of His hands as He held it marked as deep as though the stone were wax... In the midst of this church is the crown of thorns which Jesus received. And there is the lamp [by the light of which] He taught His disciples after He had supped. There is the rod [with which He was scourged] enclosed within a column of silver.'

A pilgrim record of the same period is that of the prelate Theodosius, who wrote *The Topography of the Holy Land* also in about the year 530.

From his description of Jerusalem, we find that by his day it contained no less than 26 churches, some of them not mentioned in any earlier document. We also come across a rare mention of a new festival celebrated in the Church of the Holy Sepulchre: 'From the place of Calvary it is 15 paces to Golgotha, where the cross of the Lord was found... The Invention of the Cross is observed on 14th September, the day on which it was found by Helena the mother of Constantine.' A definite date now bolstered the credibility of the event.

As to the church on Mount Zion and its pillar 'at which the Lord Christ was scourged', this pilgrim sees the marks not only of 'His arms, hands, and fingers [which] sank into it, as if it were wax', but also 'His whole countenance, His chin, nose, and eyes are imprinted on it'.

Theodosius next mentioned a new church 'outside the Galilean Gate' on the spot where 'St Stephen [the first Christian martyr] was stoned... which was built by St Eudocia, the wife of the emperor Theodosius'. The empress Eudocia was one of the most powerful of the distinguished Christian women who came to settle in Jerusalem (after being banished from the court of Byzantium) and she made a

Scenes from the life of St Jerome are depicted in this 9th century illuminated manuscript

PEREGRINUS ROMA CESSAVERAT · HIEROSALEM HEBRAEAE LEGIS HONORI[FIC]

EUSTOCHIO NECNON PAULÆ DIVINA SALUTIS · [IN]TRA HAE[C] HIERONYMO CULTUS UBIQU[E]

lasting impact on the city. She also built a magnificent palace and was responsible for extending the city wall so that it now ran further south and again enclosed, as it had in former times, Mount Zion on the west and Ophel on the east. It was also through the intercession of Eudocia that the ban on Jews was lifted and they were once more allowed to settle in Jerusalem.

As a builder of magnificent structures in the Byzantine empire, the man who might be called the Constantine of the sixth century was emperor Justinian I, the most famous of all the rulers of the eastern empire (483-565), who succeeded to the Byzantine throne in 527. Among the buildings he erected, enlarged or embellished in Palestine were the Church of the Nativity in Bethlehem and St Catherine's Monastery in Sinai, which we have mentioned earlier; a church on Mount Gerizim (above today's Nablus), the remains of which may still be seen; walls round Tiberias, parts of which still stand; and a large church on the Mount of Olives, as well as other structures in and about Jerusalem, notably the Church of St Mary. These were to be remarked upon by later pilgrims.

The last pilgrim record before the Persian capture of Jerusalem in 614 is that of Antoninus Martyr, about whom little is known beyond the fact that he left his native Placentia (Piacenza), a small town on the river Po, in about the year 570, travelling to Constantinople, Cyprus, the Syrian coast, and from there to Acco.

He is agreeably discursive, sprinkles his narration with legends and superstitions, and offers occasional tidbits of human interest. We also find him indulging – with an engaging confession of guilt – in the practice (apparently common even in early times) of leaving names or initials at holy sites. Visiting Cana, 'where our Lord was at the wedding... we reclined upon His very couch, upon which I, unworthy that I am, wrote the names of my parents.'

Antoninus also tells us what the people and the country look like. In Nazareth, after recording that 'in the synagogue there is still a book from which our Lord was set to learn A B C', and that 'the house of the Blessed Mary is [now] a basilica', he goes on: 'In the city the beauty of the Hebrew women is so great, that no more beautiful women are found among the Hebrews... And though the Hebrews have no love for Christians, yet these women are full of charity for them. This province is like a park, in corn and produce it is like Egypt; but it excels in wine and oil, fruits, and honey. Millet, too, is there unaturally tall, higher than the stature of a tall man.'

'From Nazareth we came to Mount Tabor', and he is the first pilgrim to report that 'upon it are three churches', to commemorate the Transfiguration. (The ruins of three ancient chapels may be seen on the mount today.)

From this and from his account of other biblical sites in Galilee, Samaria and Judea, it is clear that in his day most of them were already marked by shrines. On

Some of the remains of the 2nd – 3rd century synagogue of Capernaum

the north shore of the Sea of Galilee, 'we came to the city of Capernaum', site of the synagogue where Jesus taught, and 'which is now a church'. (This site holds the very interesting ruins of a second–third century synagogue which had been built close to the house of prayer which Jesus visited, and it may be this structure which Antoninus saw.) He then went to Jericho, on to Bethany, climbed the Mount of Olives, descended through Gethsemane into the Kidron valley and so entered the city of Jerusalem.

He there described the buildings, some noted for the first time and others with which we are already familiar. However, it is worth quoting a fragment on the interior of the Church of the Holy Sepulchre which he found to be now more ornate than ever, for there had been visits by countless benefactors in the almost two hundred and fifty years since its construction: 'The stone by which the tomb was closed... is adorned with gold and precious stones... its ornaments are innumerable. From iron rods hang armlets, bracelets, chains, necklaces, coronets, waistbands, sword-belts, and crowns of emperors made of gold and precious stones, and a great number of ornaments given by empresses. The whole tomb, which has the appearance of the winning-post on a race-course, is covered with silver.'

He has an interesting reference to Herod's Palace, which he calls 'The Tower of David', showing that the tradition was already established by then.

From Jerusalem our pilgrim went to Bethlehem and from there to Hebron where he saw the Cave of Machpelah, and his account of this illustrates the process whereby shrines sacred to one religion were taken over by later faiths. This burial cave of the Hebrew Patriarchs in Hebron was revered by Jews for many centuries before the birth of Christianity, and the most impressive structure on the site had been erected by Herod. By the time Antoninus visited it, part of it had been turned into a church; and centuries later, after the birth of Islam, the church was to become a mosque. Antoninus writes: 'At this place lie buried Abraham, and Isaac, and Jacob, and Sarah, and there are also the bones of Joseph. There is a basilica built with four porticoes; in the midst is an atrium without any roof; a partition runs across it, and on the one side enter Christians, and on the other, Jews.'

Apart perhaps from the narrative of Antoninus, it cannot be said that the pilgrim records of the Byzantine period match their subject in liveliness. The country was far more absorbing, as we know from historical documents. Fortunately, several later pilgrims were to prove more eloquent and discerning, and some were to offer the only picture on record of their periods. The next group were to arrive in a land with new ways and customs and structures – the land of the Moslem conquest.

Two illustrations of the Sacrifice of Isaac. Above: A 19th century silver
prayer-book binding from Galicia. Below: A 15th century Persian manuscript

3 MOHAMMED'S DREAM

In the year 614, an army of the reborn Persian empire under Chosroes II, in a victorious campaign against the Byzantine emperor Heraclius, conquered Palestine. Fourteen years later, Heraclius regained it. But continued Byzantine rule in the country was also short-lived. The followers of a new religion had arisen in Arabia, headed by its prophet Mohammed, and by the time he died in 632, they had rapidly gained ground in the Arabian peninsula. Moslem control of this territory was consolidated by Mohammed's friend and successor, Abu Bakr, and the second caliph, Omar, also a friend and disciple of Mohammed, soon carried the war to Byzantium and Persia. In 638, Omar reached Jerusalem, but there was no fighting. The Christians capitulated.

Omar did not harm Jerusalem. Nor did he molest the Christians, or deny them freedom of worship. He allowed the Jews to return. They had suffered special hardship in the final years of Byzantine rule, and when Heraclius had re-occupied the city, many had been massacred and the survivors expelled.

As a soldier, Omar was pleased that Jerusalem had been surrendered without a struggle. He was equally pleased as a Moslem, for within Jerusalem stood a site associated with a dream of Mohammed, and he would not have wished it destroyed. This was the site of the Jewish Temple.

Why should the Jewish Temple have figured in the dream of a man from the mountains of southern Arabia who had never set foot in Jerusalem? Mohammed had never seen it; but he, in common with the people of Mecca, had heard of the sacred city, just as they were familiar with many of the Jewish customs, the heroes of Jewish history and the prophets in the Jewish scriptures, both through contact with the Jewish tribes in Arabia who had settled there in the course of the exile, and through the stories and ideas brought back by the men who travelled with the great merchant caravans; for the Meccans dominated the trade between southern Arabia and the north. Mohammed had heard more when, as a boy of twelve, he had accompanied his uncle, Abu Talib, on a caravan expedition to Damascus.

On his return from this first journey to Damascus, Mohammed worked as a shepherd during his early teens, and he was much given to meditation as he roamed

A 15th century Christian pilgrim's representation of a mosque, with Moslems at prayer in the forecourt, an ablution pool (left) and scenes of fighting in the background

Mohammed's
Dream

the hills round Mecca, recapturing in solitude the excitement of the caravan trip, the meetings with new places and new people, the overheard talk with Jews and Christians about their curious faith in one God and the tales of their fabulous Holy City. He then decided to become a merchant, like many of his fellow Meccans, and at the age of about twenty, he again joined a caravan to Damascus, this time in the service of a wealthy widow named Khadijah, fifteen years his senior, whom he later married. This marriage made him an independent merchant and brought him social advancement, and for the next twenty years, he lived the life of a respected citizen of Mecca.

Arabia at this time had no coherent religion and no religious books. Mecca had its House of Allah, the temple, or Ka'bah, but within it, as objects of worship, were idols which were called 'daughters of Allah'. There was a local tradition that this house of worship had been built by Abraham, from whom the Meccans claimed descent through Ishmael. Some Meccans, however, had no patience with idolatry, and they sought to know more of the religion of the Hebrew Patriarch. Mohammed joined them. There were a few scholarly Arabs in the area, like his wife's cousin, 'who knew the Scriptures of the Jews and Christians', and from them as well as from the Jewish tribes, Mohammed and his friends, who could not read or write, learned more about monotheism and came to revere figures like Moses and David and Solomon and Jesus (all of whom were to appear in the Koran) as the prophets of Allah.

It was Mohammed's practice after his marriage to retire to a desert cave for one month in the year to spend in quiet reflection. The month chosen was Ramadan, the month of heat (hence the name of the Moslem fast), and it was during one of these retreats that he had a revelation. He heard a voice calling to him: 'Oh Mohammed! Thou art Allah's messenger, and I am Gabriel'; and there, in the sky above the horizon stood the angel Gabriel in the form of a man. Mohammed was somewhat embarrassed when he reported this to his wife Khadijah, but she had complete faith in the divine nature of the call, and encouraged him to recognize himself as the servant of Allah. He began preaching, making fiery appeals to his fellow citizens to turn from their idolatrous ways, to worship Allah, the one and true God, directly, and warning them of divine punishment should they fail to heed the words which he, as Allah's messenger, had been commanded through the angel Gabriel to transmit. Thus began the ministry of the prophet Mohammed.

It was some years later that he had another dream in which Gabriel re-appeared, this time leading a white steed named el-Burak (which means lightning). It was on the back of this animal that Mohammed, accompanied by the angel, rode through the skies to the sacred altar-rock of the Temple of Solomon in Jerusalem, and from there was caught up through the seven heavens into the presence of Allah. From the lips of Allah he received the series of commands which the faithful were to follow. The reference in the Koran to this dream of Mohammed appears

An unusual view of the interior of the Dome of the Rock, Jerusalem

in the opening verse of the seventeenth *surah* (chapter) entitled 'The Children of Israel'. It reads: 'Glorified be He who carried His servant by night from the Inviolable Place of Worship to the Far Distant Place of Worship, the neighbourhood of which We have blessed, that We might show him of Our tokens. Lo! He, only He, is the Hearer, the Seer.' The 'Inviolable Place of Worship' was later interpreted as meaning Mecca, and the 'Far Distant Place' as Jerusalem.

This was the vision which was eventually to lead to Islam's adoption of Jerusalem as its third holy city, after Mecca and Medina.

But this did not happen immediately. As Omar moved through the conquered city and made his way to the Temple site, it was with no thought of sanctifying it as a Moslem shrine. His attitude was one of respect and curiosity. He ordered the refuse to be cleared and later had a wooden mosque built within the Temple compound. That was all.

However, his name became associated with the magnificent golden-domed building which dominates Jerusalem, and to this day it is sometimes referred to as the Mosque of Omar. But it is not his structure. It was built more than fifty years later by a caliph of the Umayyad dynasty, Abd el-Malik (685-705), and its correct name is the Dome of the Rock. It rises over the rock which is said to have been the spot from which Mohammed made his dream flight to heaven. This is the traditional rock of Mount Moriah, scene of Abraham's would-be sacrifice of Isaac, and the site of the altar of Solomon's Temple.

This great Moslem shrine is the work of Byzantine architects and Greek, Egyptian and local craftsmen. It stands on the highest point of the Jewish Temple compound, which was renamed Haram esh-Sharif, 'Noble Sanctuary', by the Arabs. It was, and is, a gracious octagonal building, surmounted by a huge cupola immediately above the Rock which is supported by an inner circle of pillars. An outer ring of columns supports the roof of the ambulatory. The interior is decorated with fine mosaics. Each of the eight outer walls is graced by slender arches. There are four doors set at the points of the compass. The approach from all sides is by broad flights of steps. The structure suffered grave damage over the centuries through earthquake and fire and underwent considerable repair. It also received many decorative additions. But it is substantially the same as it was when Abd el-Malik consecrated it in 691. (The colour of the dome is also the same, but while the present effect is gained by a layer of gold-plated aluminium, Abd el-Malik is said to have used pure gold – and then ordered it to be protected by a covering of hair, wool and leather to protect the precious metal from the weather!)

By creating this dazzling structure, Abd el-Malik created Islam's third holy city and made Jerusalem a centre of Moslem pilgrimage. This was his purpose, and the motive was as much political and economic as religious. Jerusalem was within his territory, though his seat was Damascus, and he was being fiercely challenged at the time by the rival caliph, Abdulla ibn al-Zubayr, who was in possession of

Mecca and Medina. The man who held the title and power of caliph over the two holy cities of Islam, as did al-Zubayr for nine years (683-692), could exercise a powerful influence over all Moslems – including those under Umayyad rule. Indeed, the menace to Abd el-Malik eventually became so grave that an Umayyad army was sent to crush al-Zubayr, which it did in 692. But before then, el-Malik thought he could neutralize the religious (and therefore the political) influence of Mecca by establishing a rival religious centre within his own domain. It was then that he summoned the prophet's vision to his aid. Was not the Rock in Jerusalem from which Mohammed had been launched heavenwards the natural site for the supreme Moslem shrine? It was from here that he rose to meet Allah. Mecca, on the other hand, had been the city of his enemies, the scene of his attempted assassination, the place from which he had been forced to flee to Medina. His vision of Jerusalem was bound up with a drama that was wholly divine, wholly religious, spiritual, untainted by the sordidness of human strife, as at Mecca. Here, in Jerusalem, el-Malik would raise Islam's noble sanctuary.

Nor was the caliph unmindful of the economic and subsidiary political benefits that would follow. His shrine would divert Moslem pilgrimage from Mecca to Jerusalem, and the considerable revenues it brought would flow into his, and not his rival's, coffers.

Jerusalem did not become the holiest Moslem city, but the fact that its sanctity was accepted at all, even though Mohammed had never set foot in it, was a feat of no mean magnitude. The caliph could be well pleased with the measure of success his plan had achieved, and soon Moslems from all over the region were thronging to Jerusalem to gaze at his architectural masterpiece. They were to come in greater numbers a few years later after the construction of the silver-domed Mosque of El-Aksa at the southern end of the Temple compound.

This building was long credited also to Abd el-Malik, but it is now believed to have been constructed by his son, the caliph Walid, early in the eighth century. Nothing remains of the original structure beyond a few of the pillars in the colonnade to the east of the dome, and no plans have been preserved. All we know is that it was a large, solid and handsome building, and that its floor was covered with marble and its doors with silver and gold. It suffered several destructions by earthquake and underwent a number of reconstructions in the centuries that followed, a process reflected in the successive records of Moslem pilgrims. Decorative features were added by later Moslem rulers, and they also beautified the Haram esh-Sharif compound with fountains and small chapels, gates, minarets and arcades. But the two main structures in the compound, which virtually became the trademark of the city, were, and are today, the Dome of the Rock and the Mosque of El-Aksa. They would attract Moslem pilgrims from near and far, and among them would be two whose accounts of the city are among the liveliest of all the records of early travellers.

One of the eight tiled façades of the Dome of the Rock
Overleaf: Glass mosaic decoration on the drum of the Dome of the Rock

والدستور الجسور المفخّم سعادة الحاج سليمان باشا والي ايالة صيدا الوط

يد المامور بالبنا والتعمير بالامر العالي الخطير الوزير الوفور المعظم

4 ARCULF, WILLIBALD AND BERNARD THE WISE

The first record of a Christian pilgrimage after the Moslem conquest is that of a French bishop who dictated his account to a scholarly Irish abbot of a Scottish monastery. The pilgrim was Bishop Arculf; the abbot was Adamnan. The date was about 670, some thirty years after the caliph Omar entered Jerusalem. Arculf spent nine months in the country, and on his return from the east, his ship was battered by violent storms and carried by contrary winds to a little island off the west coast of Scotland, where it was wrecked. Arculf found shelter in the Monastery of Hy; and there, during the long and gloomy winter nights, he dictated his pilgrimage story to the Abbot Adamnan. The Venerable Bede (673-735), historian and theologian, known as 'the father of English history', made an abridgement of Arculf's narrative which became the textbook on pilgrimage among the English, and is credited with having led to that passion for pilgrimage with which they were soon afterwards seized.

The historical importance of Arculf's report lies in the picture it presents of the state of the Christian community in the country and of its shrines after more than a generation of Moslem occupation. The influence of the Moslems seems as yet to have been minimal – they were too busy organizing the administration of the extensive territories they had conquered and now occupied, most of them more important than Palestine. There was very little building of mosques – it was much simpler at this early stage to take over part of a church and convert it into a Moslem house of prayer. (The era of major Moslem building would begin only later in the century.) There was no sign of repression of Christians. And whatever the extent of the Persian destruction and of Moslem requisitioning, most of the churches with which we are already familiar had been repaired or rebuilt or left reasonably intact.

In Jerusalem, the restored Church of the Holy Sepulchre was still the outstanding structure in the city. Among the other churches in Jerusalem, Arculf mentioned 'the great basilica built on Mount Zion' which now commemorated not only 'the place where our Lord... was scourged', as reported by earlier pilgrims, but also 'the site of our Lord's supper' and 'the spot where the Virgin Mary died'. This is

A 7th century mosaic from an Armenian chapel in Jerusalem dedicated to the unknown Armenian soldier

one of the earliest references to Mount Zion as the scene of these events.

Churches also abounded in the rest of the country. There was a church on the river Jordan near Jericho marking the baptism of Jesus and above it the Church and Monastery of St John, and there were shrines in Shechem in Samaria and on the shores of the Sea of Galilee. In Nazareth there were 'two very large churches' commemorating the Annunciation and the site of Jesus' boyhood home, and on Mount Tabor, site of the Transfiguration, were 'three very celebrated churches of no small construction'.

There is only one item of Moslem interest in the Arculf narrative, a brief note on the temporary mosque established by Omar: 'In that renowned place where once the Temple had been magnificently constructed, placed in the neighbourhood of the wall from the east, the Saracens now frequent a four-sided house of prayer, which they have built in a rough manner by raising planks and great beams on some remains of ruins; and it is said that this house can hold three thousand men at once.'

The Dome of the Rock had not yet been built at the time of Arculf's visit. But it stood in all its glory when Bishop Willibald, our next pilgrim, reached Jerusalem, yet his record is innocent of any reference to it. This is characteristic of most accounts by the early Christian pilgrims, which are concerned exclusively with the Christian holy places, but later Moslem travellers would be filling the gaps.

Willibald, an Englishman of noble rank, journeyed to the Holy Land as a young man in the year 721, and one reference in the account of his visits to the usual churches and shrines is of special interest for the light it throws on the development of Christian pilgrimage. In the Church of the Ascension on the Mount of Olives, he saw 'two columns standing within', and he was told that 'the man who can creep between the wall and the columns will have remission of his sins'. Here is one of the earliest mentions of a concept which was to grow in importance and play a decisive role in the ideology of the Crusades – the concept of pilgrimage as a means of gaining a plenary indulgence.

Willibald visited another site which would be on the itinerary of future pilgrims and which still excites the modern traveller to Israel. Journeying through the Judean wilderness visiting hermits and monks, he came to 'a large monastery' where he met 'the numerous monks who dwell in little cells cut out in the stony rock of the mountain here and there... and there rests St Sabba'. (St Sabba, founder of the monastery in 483, was archimandrite over all the monks of Palestine.) The Monastery of Mar Sabba, clinging to the rock above the wadi in the heart of forbidding desert, underwent many reconstructions, though its immediate surroundings have remained comparatively untouched, and the adjoining slopes are pitted with natural and man-made recesses. It presents the same dramatic sight today as it did when Willibald came upon it in the eighth century.

In these years immediately following the Moslem conquest, Christian and Jewish pilgrims, though much harassed on their journeys, were allowed to visit their shrines. This was the overall policy (though the policy of local chieftains often conflicted with it) laid down by the Moslem rulers. Their attitude to the practice of 'infidel' pilgrimage was ambivalent: they abhorred it on religious grounds but welcomed the revenues it brought. The balance of the ambivalence varied with the character of the reigning caliph. The renowned Haroun el-Rashid (786-809), the most noted of the Abbasid rulers, for example, gave specific recognition of the universal Christian interest in Jerusalem when he allowed the great Charlemagne, emperor of the West, to endow and maintain centres in the city for western pilgrims.

Curiously enough, the ones who were critical of el-Rashid's action were not so much the ultra-orthodox Moslems as the Eastern Christians. From early times there had been conflict between the Eastern (Greek Orthodox) and Western (Latin) Churches, and the rivalry, though not as intense, continues to this day. The Jerusalem patriarch was thus deeply disturbed when Charlemagne secured rights for the Western Church from the caliph.

Palestine, then, was a Moslem territory ruled by the caliphate in the north, first from Syria and then from Iraq. In 877, it was brought within the sphere of southern Moslem rule after one of the Abbasid officials in Egypt, Ahmad ibn-Tulun, declared himself the independent governor of Egypt and extended his sway over the Holy Land.

It was shortly before this, in 870, that the last Christian pilgrim of whom we have a record before the Crusader period visited the country. He was a Breton monk known as Bernard the Wise, and his account reflects the weakened central authority in Baghdad and the growing power of local Moslem rulers. He set out with two fellow monks. They went first to Rome for the Pope's blessing and then proceeded to southern Italy from where they were to set sail. At Bari, which was under Moslem control, they secured letters of protection from the local sultan to his Moslem counterparts in Alexandria and Babylon (the Egyptian city, site of Old Cairo, not to be confused with the famous Babylon of Mesopotamia). They left for Alexandria, 'the voyage lasting thirty days', and their first troubles began. 'Wishing to go ashore we were prevented by the captain of the crew, who was in command of sixty men. However, in order that opportunity might be given us to disembark, we gave him six gold pieces.' They were to become less felicitous about 'opportunities' gained by bribery as they proceeded.

They went directly 'to the prince of Alexandria and showed him the letter which the sultan had given us; but it availed us nothing, although he admitted that he was not ignorant of the contents of the letter. As he pressed us, we gave him, each of us, 300 denarii for himself; and then he wrote letters for us to the prince of Babylon.' They then took a barge down the Nile, 'sailing to the south six days', and when they stepped ashore at Babylon, 'the guards of the city carried us before the prince who enquired of us the object of our journey, and asked us from what princes we had letters. Whereupon we showed him the letters of the aforesaid sultan and those of the prince of Alexandria; but they were of no service to us, for he sent us to prison, where we remained six days, and then it occurred to us by the help of God to give him 300 denarii each as in the former case, and we obtained our liberty.'

When they reached Jerusalem, Bernard and his companions were able to profit from the Charlemagne—el-Rashid agreement. 'We arrived at the holy city, and were received into the hostel of the most glorious emperor Charles, where all are admitted who come to this place for devotional reasons, and speak the Roman tongue. Close to it is a church in honour of St Mary, which has a noble library through the care of the aforesaid emperor, with twelve dwelling houses, fields, vineyards and a garden in the Valley of Jehoshaphat. Before the hostel is the market...' This, incidentally, is the only account on record of Charlemagne's foundations in Jerusalem.

Bernard reports an interesting ritual which is mentioned by no previous writer, though it is often referred to by subsequent pilgrims. It takes place in the Church of the Holy Sepulchre. 'On Holy Saturday, which is the eve of Easter, the office is begun early in this church, and after it is ended, the *Kyrie Eleison* is chanted, until an angel comes and lights the lamps that hang above the aforesaid sepulchre. The patriarch gives this fire to the bishops and to the rest of the people, that each may with it light up his own house.'

This ceremony of the 'Holy Fire' was a celebrated miracle in the Middle Ages – the ritual is still practised by the Greek Orthodox Church – and it gave rise to a story that the allegation of trickery behind the ritual was what angered the caliph al-Hakim (996–1021) – or was used as a pretext by him – so that he had the Church of the Holy Sepulchre destroyed (in 1008). The story is told by an Eastern Christian writer named Abulfaragius: 'The author of this persecution was some enemy of the Christians, who told Hakim that, when the Christians assembled in their temple at Jerusalem, to celebrate Easter, the chaplains of the church, making use of a pious fraud, greased the chain of iron that held the lamp over the tomb with oil of balsam; and that, when the Arab officer had sealed up the door which led to the tomb, they applied a match, through the roof, to the other extremity of the chain, and the fire descended immediately to the wick of the lamp and lighted it. Then the worshippers burst into tears, and cried out *Kyrie Eleison*, supposing it was fire which fell from heaven upon the tomb; and they were thus strengthened in their faith.'

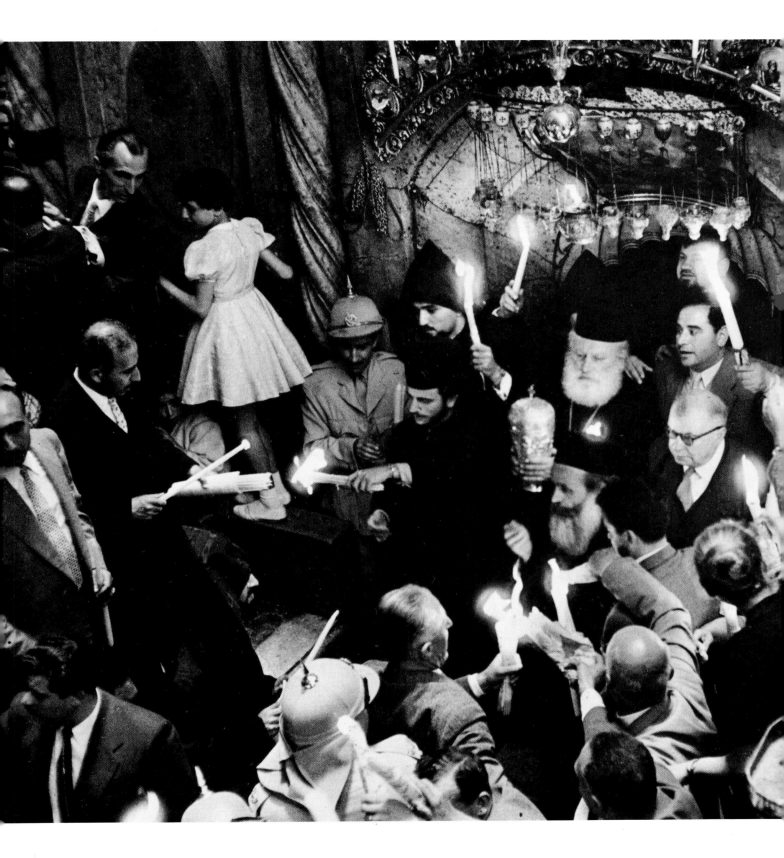

A 1966 photograph of the ceremony of the 'Holy Fire' in the Church of the Holy Sepulchre

The Monastery of Mar Sabba in the Judean wilderness

The refectory of Mar Sabba

5 MUKADDASI AND NASIR THE SON OF KHUSRAU

The freshest and liveliest account of what the people and the country were like towards the end of Arab rule, little more than a century before the Crusades (and a few years before the destructive action of the caliph Hakim), is undoubtedly that of the Moslem traveller Mukaddasi, who published his work in 985. His real name was Shams ad Din Abu Abd Allah Mohammed, but he is known as Mukaddasi – 'He who comes from the Holy City'.

His account of Palestine began with the north, and the first town he mentioned was Tiberias, noted for its hot sulphur springs, on the western shore of the Sea of Galilee. This was the city built in the first century AD by Herod Antipas, tetrarch of Galilee and son of Herod the Great, and named in honour of the Roman emperor Tiberius. After the destruction of Jerusalem, it became the seat of Jewish learning and the dwelling place of great sages, whose greatest work there was the codification of the traditional Jewish jurisprudence, the Mishnah, at the end of the second century. Some of the most venerated sites of antiquity (to this day) are the tombs of these Jewish scholars from the first, second and third centuries (though the most noted site would be the early thirteenth century tomb of Rabbi Moses ben Maimon [Maimonides], the greatest Jewish scholar of his age).

Mukaddasi's brief but mordant description of Tiberias is characteristic. In his treatment of each town, he presented its salient qualities. If he liked a place, he could enthuse; if he disliked it, he could be scathing in an engaging way. Tiberias is below sea level, and Mukaddasi must have visited it in summer when it is hot and sticky. He did not like Tiberias. This is what he wrote: 'The houses stand between the mountain and the Lake. It is narrow, shut in in summer, and unhealthy. The town is nearly a league in length, but has no breadth. Its market-place extends from one city gate to the other, and its graveyard is on the hill slope. There are here eight natural hot-baths, where no fuel need be used, and numberless basins besides, of boiling water. The mosque is large and fine, and stands in the market-place. Its floor is laid in pebbles set on stone drums placed close one to another. Of the people of Tiberias is it said: that for two months they dance, and for two more they gorge, that for two months they beat about, and for two more they

The domed shrine in Tiberias of Rabbi Meir Ba'al Haness, 2nd century AD
Jewish scholar, 'giver of light' and 'maker of miracles'

go naked, that for two months they play the reed, and for two more they wallow. The explanation of this is, that they dance from the number of the fleas, then gorge off the Nabak plum [a sweet fruit, the size of a medlar, with many kernels]; they beat about with fly-flaps to chase away the wasps from the meat and the fruits, then they go naked from the heat; they suck the sugar-canes, and then they have to wallow through their muddy streets.'

Moving through hilly Upper Galilee, he found 'there are many fine villages, and here are grown grapes and other fruits and olives'. He continued westwards to biblical Acco (which the Crusaders would later rename Acre). 'Acco', he wrote, 'is a fortified city on the sea. The mosque here is very large. In its court is a clump of olive trees, the oil from which suffices for the lamps of the mosque, and yet besides. This city had remained unfortified until the time when Ibn Tulun visited it, coming from Tyre, where he had seen the fortifications and the walls which are there carried round so as to protect the harbour. Ibn Tulun wished to construct at Acco a fortification that should be as impregnable as that of Tyre.' And he succeeded. 'Now before this harbour had been made the enemy were wont to take advantage of the ships lying here and do them grievous damage.'

Mukaddasi then travelled south to Ramla, which is roughly midway along today's Tel-Aviv–Jerusalem main road, and his is the first account we have of the only town ever built in Palestine by the Moslems. It was founded in 716 by the caliph Suleiman (715-717), son of the celebrated Abd el-Malik who built the Dome of the Rock and brother of Walid who built the Mosque of El-Aksa. Suleiman was the only caliph to make Palestine his country of residence, and he resolved to build himself a new capital on a totally new site. The location he chose was close to Lod (Lydda), the biblical city commanding the junction of two great caravan routes, which had served the Moslems as the capital of the province. His new city would replace it, assume its strategic function and enjoy its economic benefits as a market town on the trading highways. Part of Lod was demolished and its people were re-settled in the new city. Suleiman applied himself vigorously to creating what he hoped would be a great city, beginning the building of a fortress, a handsome mosque and a palace, establishing economic enterprises and securing its water supply by conduit from distant sources. His work was carried on by his successors.

The most notable of their later constructions was the magnificent, arched, underground cistern built towards the end of the eighth century by the caliph Haroun el-Rashid. [It was discovered only recently and it is beautifully preserved. It is, indeed, exactly as it was when it was built. A stone staircase leads to its base from which giant columns rise to form twenty-four arched bays, each with an aperture in its dome from which the water was drawn and which is now glassed in. Today, a small boat awaits the visitor at the foot of the steps, and in it one can paddle between the pillars and inspect the interesting stonework round the bays.]

(It is of no mean significance that not only did no other Moslem emperor live

74   The ancient hot springs of Tiberias

in Palestine, and Suleiman himself for his reign of less than three years, but it never occurred either to him or to any other Moslem leader who preceded or came after him to make Jerusalem the capital. Not even Abd el-Malik had done so, and despite his success in vesting Jerusalem with a sanctity for Islam, it could never mean as much to Moslems as it did, and does, to Jews and Christians. In 1948, more than twelve centuries after Suleiman proclaimed the new city of Ramla as his capital, half of a divided Jerusalem fell within the control of the Moslem king of Jordan, and remained so for nineteen years, right up to the Six Day War of 1967; yet he maintained his rule from Amman as his capital city. The Jews alone had restored their half of the city as the capital of Israel.)

Ramla had risen on a virgin stretch of sand – *raml* means sand in Arabic – and Mukaddasi was visiting it more than two hundred and fifty years after its establishment. He opens by itemising the city's virtues: 'Ramla is the capital of Palestine. It is a fine city, and well built; its water is good and plentiful; its fruits are abundant. It combines manifold advantages, situated as it is in the midst of beautiful villages and lordly towns, near to the holy places and pleasant hamlets. Commerce here is prosperous, and means of livelihood easy. There is no finer mosque in Islam than the one in the city; its bread is of the best and the whitest; its lands are well favoured above all others, and its fruits are of the most luscious... It possesses magnificent hostelries and pleasant baths, dainty food and various condiments, spacious houses, fine mosques and broad roads... Its disadvantages, on the other hand, are, that in winter the place is a slough of mud, while in summer it is a powder-box of sand, where no water flows, neither is anything green, nor is the soil humid, nor is there snow. Fleas here abound. The chief mosque of Ramla is in the market, and it is even more beautiful and graceful than that of Damascus. It is called Al Abyad [the White Mosque].' (Fragmentary relics of this mosque, which was rebuilt by Saladin at the end of the twelfth century, may be seen today at the foot of the 'White Tower', Ramla's most prominent landmark). 'In all Islam there is found no finer mihrab than the one here. [The *mihrab* is the niche reserved for the imam who leads the prayer, and it marks the *kibla*, the direction of Mecca.] Its pulpit is the most exquisite that is to be seen after that of Jerusalem; also it possesses a beautiful minaret, built by the Caliph Hisham [724-743].'

Mukaddasi then reached Jerusalem: 'The buildings of the Holy City are of stone, and you will find nowhere finer or more solid constructions. In no place will you meet with a people more chaste... Wine is not publicly consumed, and there is no drunkenness. The city is devoid of houses of ill-fame, whether public or private. The people too are noted for piety and sincerity... Provisions are most excellent here, the markets are clean, the mosque is the largest, and nowhere are Holy Places more numerous. The grapes are enormous, and there are no quinces to equal those of the Holy City... All the year round, never are her streets empty of strangers.'

At this point in his narrative, he apparently senses that he is being too uncritical,

The 13th century White Tower of Ramla

and so he goes on: 'Still, Jerusalem has some disadvantages. Thus... learned men are few, and the Christians numerous, and the same are unmannerly in the public places. In the hostelries taxes are heavy on all that is sold... Erudite men have no renown; also the schools are unattended, for there are no lectures. Everywhere the Christians and the Jews have the upper hand; and the mosque is void of either congregation or assembly of learned men.'

Next comes Mukaddasi's description of the Haram esh-Sharif, the Mosque of El-Aksa and the Dome of the Rock, and he says quite openly that the intention was to rival the Christian buildings in splendour. This mosque compound, he writes, 'is even more beautiful than that of Damascus, for during the building of it they had for a rival and as a comparison the great church [of the Holy Sepulchre] belonging to the Christians at Jerusalem, and they built this to be even more magnificent than that other'.

Of the Mosque of El-Aksa, he says that 'in the days of the Abbasids occurred the earthquakes which threw down most of the main building; all, in fact, except that portion round the mihrab.' The reigning caliph then ordered each provincial governor and commander to 'undertake the building of a colonnade... and the edifice rose firmer and more substantial than ever it had been in former times...'

The large Haram esh-Sharif court 'is paved in all parts; in its centre rises a platform, like that of the mosque at Medina, to which, from all four sides, ascend broad flights of steps', and he lists the smaller structures that now stand there, the gifts of members of successive ruling families who followed the custom of beautifying Moslem shrines. This brings him to the Haram's noblest edifice:

'In the centre of the platform is the Dome of the Rock, which rises above an octagonal building having four gates... all adorned with gold, and closing each of them is a beautiful door of cedar-wood finely worked in pattern...'

'At the dawn, when the light of the sun first strikes on the Cupola, and the Drum catches the rays; then is this edifice a marvellous sight to behold, and one such that in all Islam I have never seen its equal; neither have I heard tell of aught built in pagan times that could rival in grace this Dome of the Rock.'

Of other towns in the country, he offered only a brief note on Bethlehem – 'Jesus was born here' – but gives a long description of Hebron, because of its association with the Hebrew Patriarch Abraham who is revered by the Moslems as Al-Khalil, 'the Friend of God'. (This, indeed, is the Arabic name of Hebron to this day.) By the time of Mukaddasi's visit, the Cave of the Patriarchs, whom the Moslems have taken over as prophets, has been turned into a mosque. He writes: 'Within it [Hebron] is a strong fortress... being of great squared stones. In the middle of this place rises the Dome built... of stone, which covers the sepulchre of Abraham. The tomb of Isaac lies forward, within the main building of the mosque, while that of Jacob is in the further part...'

Of Gaza we learn little other than that it is still 'a large town lying on the

The interior of the Mosque of El-Aksa showing the ornate pulpit destroyed by fire in 1968

highroad into Egypt, on the border of the desert', and that 'there is here a beautiful mosque'. By now, the mosque is a feature of every settlement in the country.

He is more taken by Ashkelon, which is 'a fine city, and strongly garrisoned. Fruit is here in plenty... The silkworms of this place are renowned, its wares are excellent, and life there is pleasant.'

Jaffa, surprisingly, was 'but a small town', even though it was 'the emporium of Palestine and the port of Ramla. It is protected by an impregnable fortress, with iron gates; and the sea-gates are also of iron.' Of Caesarea, however, he says that 'there is no city more beautiful, nor any better filled with good things... Its lands are excellent, and its fruits delicious; the town is also famous for its buffalo-milk and its white bread.'

In his account of Jericho, there is a strange absence of any mention of the magnificent winter palace built there by the Umayyad caliph Hisham ibn Abd el-Malik (724-743), who also built the minaret and other constructions in Ramla. The probable reason is that the palace was never occupied, for most of its buildings collapsed shortly after their completion in the great earthquake of 747 and were not rebuilt. When Mukaddasi visited the town more than a century later, the ruins may have been covered by debris, or he may have thought ruins not worth recording. However, this sumptuous structure, a huge walled estate complete with colonnaded courts, ornamental pool, mosque, lavish residential quarters, bath-houses, and remarkable mosaic floors and decorative stone-work, was recently excavated. A handsome restoration was completed in 1968.

Mukaddasi ends his narrative with a miscellaneous rag-bag of informative tidbits which round off his presentation of the products and beauties of the land and the manner and customs of the people.

He bemoans the fact that there are no Moslem philosophers or intellectuals of serious worth, 'or that any Moslem here is the writer of aught; except only at Tiberias, where the scribes have ever been in repute'.

He gives the country's main exports: 'From Palestine come olives, dried figs, raisins, the carob-fruit, stuffs of mixed silk and cotton, soaps and kerchiefs.' He singles out Jerusalem, from which come 'cheeses, cotton, raisins... excellent apples, bananas – which same is a fruit of the form of a cucumber, but the skin peels off and the interior is not unlike the water-melon, only finer flavoured and more luscious – also pine-nuts... mirrors, lamp-jars, and needles... The best honey is that from Jerusalem, where the bees suck the thyme.'

One final extract from Mukaddasi, written in a straightforward manner about incidents which were an accepted every-day occurrence, evokes the flavour of uncertain life in tenth century Palestine – the constant fear of attack, the agitated response to an alarm, and the matter-of-fact commerce in prisoners taken in frequent battle. This was the atmosphere encountered by the pilgrims of those days.

Mukaddasi wrote: 'All along the coast [of Palestine] are the watch-stations where the levies assemble. The warships and the galleys of the Greeks also come into these ports, bringing aboard of them the captives taken from the Moslems; these they offer for ransom – three for the hundred Dinars. And in each of these ports there are men who know the Greek tongue, for they... trade with them in divers wares. At the stations, whenever a Greek vessel appears, they sound the horns; also if it be night they light a beacon there, on the tower, or, if it be day, they make a great smoke. From every watch-station on the coast up to the capital [Ramla] are built, at intervals, high towers, in each of which is stationed a company of men. On the occasion of the arrival of the Greek ships the men, perceiving them, kindle the beacon on the tower nearest to the coast station, and then on that lying next above it, and then on, one after another; so that hardly is an hour elapsed before the trumpets are sounding in the capital, and drums are beating in the towers, calling the people down to their watch-station by the sea; and they hurry out in force, with their arms, and the young men of the villages gather together. [For they do not know whether the ships have come on a peaceful or warlike mission.] Then the ransoming begins. One prisoner will be given in exchange for another [for the Moslems on their part have western captives], or money and jewels will be offered; until at length all the prisoners who are in the Greek ships have been set free. And the watch-stations where this ransoming of captives takes place are' – among others – 'Gaza, Ashkelon and Jaffa.'

Mukaddasi was writing about the country during the opening years of Fatimid rule. The Fatimids (claiming descent from Fatima, daughter of Mohammed) had conquered Egypt in 969 and gone on to take Palestine. At first, life for Christians and Jews was comparatively uneventful. But when al-Hakim became caliph in 996, he launched a policy of harsh persecution of the 'infidels', trying to convert them to Islam by force and denying them places of worship by destroying their churches and synagogues. It was at this time that the Church of the Holy Sepulchre was demolished. This act was to be recalled time and again throughout the following century to add fuel to that mood among the Christians in the west which was to lead to the Crusades, even though the reconstruction of the Sepulchre was allowed by Hakim's successors and was begun in 1037, some thirty years after its destruction, in the reign of caliph al-Mustansir (in return for the release by Byzantium of five thousand Moslem prisoners).

Work on the church was sufficiently advanced by the year 1047 to have impressed another Moslem traveller, who on arrival in Jerusalem made the following entry in his diary: 'The Christians possess a church which they call the Church of the Resurrection, and they hold it in great veneration... At the present day the church is a most spacious building, and is capable of containing eight thousand persons. The edifice is built, with the utmost skill, of coloured marble, with ornamentation and sculptures. Inside, the church is everywhere adorned with Byzantine brocade, worked in gold with pictures.'

Another view of the Mosque of El-Aksa, some 80 years ago

A tomb in the Cave of the Patriarchs, Hebron

The writer was Nasir-l-Khusrau (Nasir the son of Khusrau), and he is the last pilgrim before the Crusader period whose record has been preserved. (He wrote in Persian, and the extracts we use are taken from the translation in 1893 by the British orientalist, Guy le Strange, who also translated from the original Arabic the extracts from Mukaddasi given earlier in this chapter.)

Nasir-l-Khusrau was an engaging character, a man of letters, a distinguished civil servant – and a reformed drunkard. Born near the Persian-Afghan frontier into a noble Moslem family, he rose to a high position in the service of a local sultan or governor, on whose behalf he travelled much through the rugged country of Afghanistan and northern India. It was no doubt during the icy nights at stop-over posts on remote trading routes, where the merchants from Samarkand and other exotic places would foregather, that he became addicted, as he confesses in his diary-narrative, to the 'pleasures of the wine-cup', forbidden to Moslems. One night, after imbibing heavily, he fell into a stupor and was tormented by a guilt-laden dream, in which he was admonished by a pious apparition to mend his ways while there was still time. When he awoke, he determined to repent and forthwith to make the pilgrimage to Mecca. He concluded his affairs, returned home, secured his release from the governor's service, and started off on a more than 3,000 mile trek, much of it over mountainous country. He travelled through the northwestern provinces of Persia, Azerbaijan, Armenia and Mesopotamia, crossed the Euphrates, and proceeded west through Syria and Lebanon until he reached the Mediterranean. He then turned south into Palestine, entering it near Acco. Since Jerusalem lay close to his route south to Mecca, he visited it first, arriving there one year after he had left home. Although, like Mukaddasi, he was concerned primarily with Moslem sites, he did mention the outstanding Jewish and Christian places he came across, and the Church of the Holy Sepulchre was among the first.

He was familiar with its recent history, and he wrote that 'Hakim at one time ordered the church to be given over to plunder, which was so done, and it was laid in ruins. Some time it remained thus; but afterwards the caesar of Byzantium sent ambassadors with presents and promises of service, and concluded a treaty in which he stipulated for permission to defray the expenses of rebuilding the church, and this was ultimately accomplished.'

In his day, as we learn from his record, Christians and Jews were again allowed to make the pilgrimage to Jerusalem. This confirms what we know from other sources that in the fifty years or so after the death of Hakim, there was a considerable movement of Christians pilgrims from the west, while Jews from towns and villages in the rest of Palestine as well as from the Diaspora communities visited Jerusalem on one or other of the Pilgrim Festivals. Nasir-l-Khusrau wrote: 'From all the countries of the Greeks and from other lands, the Christians and the Jews come up to Jerusalem in great numbers in order to make their visitation of the Church [of the Holy Sepulchre] and the Synagogue that is there.'

As for Moslem pilgrimage, he showed that it was mostly those who 'are unable to make the pilgrimage to Mecca [who] will go up at the appointed season to Jerusalem... There are years when as many as twenty thousand people will be present at Jerusalem during the first days of the pilgrimage month... for they bring their children also with them in order to celebrate their circumcision.'

We then learn from him the almost precise degree of success Abd el-Malik had finally achieved in making Jerusalem a holy city for Islam; for our eleventh century pilgrim records the prevailing estimate of the comparative ratings of sanctity for the three sacred Moslem cities: 'The Noble Sanctuary [in Jerusalem] is the third of the Houses of God, and the doctors of religion concur in saying that a single prayer offered up here, in this Holy City, has vouchsafed to it the effect of five-and-twenty thousand prayers said elsewhere; just as in Medina... every single prayer may count for fifty thousand; while each that is said in Mecca... will pass for a hundred thousand.'

During the seven-year pilgrimage wanderings of Nasir-l-Khusrau, a new power had arisen in the region of his birthplace and was rapidly driving westwards, across much of the territory he had traversed as a pilgrim. This was the army of the Seljuks, an outlying branch of the Turks, who came from the far eastern provinces of Islam, close to the borders of China. They had been converted to Islam while serving as mercenaries to the Moslem rulers of Persia and northwest India, and they had subsequently overthrown their masters. By 1055, they had swept into Baghdad, and five years later had overrun Syria. In 1071 they drove the Fatimids from the northern half of Palestine, including Jerusalem, and ruled it for the next twenty-five years. In 1076, there was a rebellion in Jerusalem, and the Seljuks suppressed it vigorously, massacring many of its inhabitants, destroying buildings, and introducing a policy of repression against the surviving Christians and Jews. Pilgrimage was banned, and pilgrims who happened to be there at the time were gravely maltreated. The effect on the Christian world was to stiffen their determination to launch a counter-offensive. While the first Christian troops were on their way to the Holy Land, the Seljuks and Fatimids were again locked in battle – with the Fatimids regaining Jerusalem. It was largely because these two Moslem powers were too busy fighting each other to present a common front against the Christian army from the west that the Crusaders were able to reach Syria with comparative ease in 1098. On 15 July 1099, they captured Jerusalem, and established the Crusader kingdom.

18th century print of the Church of the Holy Sepulchre from a Russian guide-book for pilgrims

И къ востоку ꙗкѡ верженїе камене ѿ палатахъ дв҃двыхъ,
ѐсть великїй, и преславный храмъ ст҃агѡ гроба гдⷭ҇на пре,
красный, и круговидный, имѣꙗй трꙋлли три во ѡбра
ст҃ыꙗ трⷪ҇цы, и ꙁвоницꙋ краснѣйшꙋ и высокꙋ: имѣꙗше сей
храмъ первѣе вратъ седмъ, ѿ нихже ѐдина точїю сꙋтъ ѿво
ренна на полꙋдни
Іерⷧ҇лимꙋ.

Храмъ
преⷭ҇: Гроба.

И вхⷪ҇

6 THE CRUSADER KINGDOM

The idea of the Crusades had been launched by Pope Urban II at a specially summoned Church Council in Clermont (France) in November 1095. After the routine ecclesiastical deliberations held in the cathedral, the Pope called for a public session at which he would make an important announcement. A large field outside Clermont's city gates was prepared, the papal throne installed on a high dais, and when the Council churchmen and the vast numbers of the lay public were assembled, Urban rose and made an impassioned exhortation on the merit and glory of delivering the Holy Land from the hands of its desecrators, coupled with a powerful call to arms. The response was overwhelming.

There were forceful Christian reasons expounded by the Pope which drew this response – the harsh treatment of non-Moslems by the Seljuks; the ban on pilgrimage; the appeal for help by Byzantium, the hard-pressed defenders of Christianity (and territory) against the encroachment of non-Christian Asians. But there were other factors which helped to transform an appeal at a public gathering into a practical military Crusade. The circumstances were propitious. Western Europe was in a state of expansion. There were navies to carry the men and equipment, and such commercial ports as Venice, Genoa and Pisa, with their fleets, could look to increased trade with the eastern Mediterranean. Moreover, the class of knightly warriors produced by the new social order in Europe was only too eager to gain new domains for itself. As Gibbon observes in *The Decline and Fall of the Roman Empire*, 'In the petty quarrels of Europe they shed the blood of their friends and countrymen for the acquisition, perhaps, of a castle or a village. [Now] they could march with alacrity against the distant and hostile nations... Their fancy already grasped the golden sceptres of Asia... The vulgar, both the great and small, were taught to believe every wonder, of lands flowing with milk and honey, of mines and treasures, of gold and diamonds, of palaces of marble and jaspar, and of odoriferous groves of cinammon and frankincense. In this earthly paradise each warrior depended on his sword to carve a plenteous and honourable establishment, which he measured only by the extent of his wishes.'

Added to all this, enlistment in the Crusades carried with it a plenary indulgence

Model of a pilgrim boat of the Crusader period in the Maritime Museum, Haifa

– the absolution of *all* sin and a full receipt for *all* that might be due of canonical penance. We have seen from the pilgrim Willibald how pilgrimage began to be associated with the remission of sin. This factor was of special importance at this time, for, in Gibbon's words, 'as the manners of the Christians were relaxed, their discipline of penance was enforced; and with the multiplication of sins the remedies were multiplied'. Now, by following the banner of the cross, guilt was wiped out and all could suddenly be vested with both piety and courage. Thus, 'at the voice of their pastor, the robber, the incendiary, the homicide arose by thousands to redeem their souls by repeating on the infidels the same deeds which they had exercised against their Christian brethren'; and if they fell in battle, 'the spirit of the Latin clergy did not hesitate to adorn their tomb with the crown of martyrdom'.

This, then, was the background to the decision of the Church Council at Clermont. What Pope Urban and the princes planned and eventually carried out was a well directed invasion by picked armies. But what immediately followed, in 1096, was the Peasants' Crusade, the undisciplined march of hundreds of thousands of 'thoughtless and needy plebeians across Europe, massacring Jews and plundering the property of Gentiles en route, and leaving widespread ruin in their wake. They were led by fanatical monks and preachers, notably Peter the Hermit (Peter of Picardy), a volatile pilgrim who had been molested by the Seljuks and who had returned to the west to rouse churchmen to undertake a holy war and rescue Christian sanctuaries from the infidel. Behind him and other rabble-rousers there followed about 300,000, in Gibbon's estimate – 'the most stupid and savage refuse of the people, who mingled with their devotion a brutal licence of rapine, prostitution, and drunkenness'. As they moved through Europe, they undertook, stated Gibbon, 'the first and most easy warfare – against the Jews... In the trading cities of the Moselle and the Rhine... at Verdun, Treves, Mentz, Spires, Worms, many thousands of that unhappy people were pillaged and massacred, nor had they felt a more bloody stroke since the persecution of Hadrian.'

The followers of this Peasants' Crusade never reached the Holy Land. Most of them perished before even setting foot in Asia Minor. They were killed or turned back and left to starve by Christian communities situated along the later stages of their route, who had heard of their ruinous depredations. It was the official armies led by the knights who constituted the First Crusade, carefully preparing their military enterprise before moving east in the following year, launching their successful invasion of Syria and establishing themselves there before driving southwards into Palestine.

When they captured Jerusalem, the Crusader forces went on a rampage through the city, killing all Moslems and Jews whom they encountered. (The Christian residents had been ordered by the Fatimid governor to leave when he had learned of the approach of the Crusaders.) It was thus through a deserted Jerusalem that

Left, above: Detail of a frieze in the Greek Orthodox Patriarchate, Jerusalem. Below: Detail of a sculptured lintel over a door of the Church of the Holy Sepulchre. (Now in the Rockefeller Museum)

Right: A Crusader capital in the Coenaculum on Mount Zion

the Crusading princes made their thanksgiving procession to the Church of the Holy Sepulchre two days later. They were headed by the overall commander of the conquering troops, Godfrey de Bouillon, Duke of Lorraine, who became the secular and military ruler with the title of Defender of the Holy Sepulchre. Only a year later, with his death, was the royal title bestowed – upon his brother, who thus became king Baldwin I, the first head of the Crusader Kingdom of Jerusalem.

At first the size of this kingdom was small indeed, covering little more than a strip of territory linking Jerusalem and Bethlehem, via Ramla, with the coast at Jaffa. Over the next few decades, there would be almost continuous fighting to extend the Crusader foothold. First would come the battles for the coastal towns, and most of these would be captured during the early years with the aid of the Venetian, Genoese and Pisan fleets (which would later earn their patron cities considerable trade and other privileges). The expansion of Crusader control inland would take longer, and with the aim of consolidating its position, a chain of formidable castles would be constructed commanding the frontiers and main lines of communications. (The impressive ruins of many may be seen today.)

Wherever the Crusader writ would run, ecclesiastical buildings would be erected: churches, monasteries, convents and hospices for pilgrims, all of them solid and handsome. (Some are beautifully preserved.) The first step would be to rebuild the central Christian shrine, the Church of the Holy Sepulchre, and in the course of the next fifty years it would be completely reconstructed. Of the numerous other Jerusalem churches built or rebuilt by the Crusaders, the most notable (and the best preserved) would be the Church of St Anne, constructed over part of Herod's Antonia Fortress just outside the northwestern corner of the Temple compound.

All this was in the future. In the first few years, security – which would always be the Crusaders' prime problem – was their all-absorptive concern. With the Saracens holding a large stretch of the coast and most of the inland regions, communications within the Crusader enclave were unsafe, and pilgrimage to Jerusalem was fraught with risk. Nevertheless, as we learn from Fulcher of Chartres, the most reliable chronicler of the First Crusade, a trickle of pilgrims from the west began arriving in the country not long after the enthronement of Baldwin, and in 1101, he wrote, with 'the land routes still completely obstructed to our pilgrims... Franks, Angles, Italians and Venetians... with from one to four ships came timidly by sea to Joppa (Jaffa), the Lord leading them as they sailed through the midst of hostile pirates and past cities of the Saracens'.

By 1102 they were coming in greater numbers, as we learn from the record of the Anglo-Saxon pilgrim Saewulf, who landed at Jaffa in October of that year, and spoke of 'thirty very large ships, all laden with pilgrims or merchandise' having arrived at about the same time. (He adds that twenty-three of them were 'dashed against each other and broken into small pieces' when a mighty gale struck the port as they were coming in or just as they had cast anchor, and 'more than a thousand persons of either sex perished on that day'.)

Little is known of Saewulf beyond the fact that he was a merchant given to indulging the temptations of a roving life who would every so often repair to Bishop Wulstan of Worcester to confess his sins. The good bishop would urge him to forsake his old courses and embrace the monastic life, but the pattern would be repeated. Shortly after the road to Jerusalem had been laid open by the first Crusader successes, Saewulf again paid a penitential visit to his clerical friend. The result was his departure on pilgrimage.

The anxieties of travel along the insecure roads even within Crusader territory are well described by this early Crusader pilgrim: 'We went up from Joppa to the city of Jerusalem, a journey of two days, along a mountainous road, rocky, and very dangerous. For the Saracens, always laying snares for the Christians, lie hidden in the hollow places of the mountains, and the caves of the rocks, watching day and night, and always on the lookout for those whom they can attack on account of the fewness of the party, or those who have lagged behind their party through weariness... Oh, what a number of human bodies, both in the road and by the side of it' – of pilgrims killed or sick and left to die, and whose corpses were then 'all torn by wild beasts!'

As a description of the country at this time, Saewulf's account is not very absorbing – his journey is more exciting than his arrival. However, his report is important to historians for its record of the sacred structures which were still in existence, and although there had been a good deal of destruction, most of the well-known ones were intact. In Jerusalem, the Church of the Holy Sepulchre was still the most impressive Christian shrine (though much outshone by the Dome of the Rock which had escaped serious damage), but it was more modest than it had ever been – work on its reconstruction had not yet started. In Bethlehem 'nothing has been left habitable by the Saracens' except the Church of the Nativity. In Hebron, the building above the Cave of Machpelah still stood, and 'the monuments of the holy patriarchs, set up in ancient times, are surrounded by a very strong rampart'. In Nazareth, he sees the Church of the Annunciation, and at Mount Tabor 'the three monasteries anciently built on its summit still exist'. On the Sea of Galilee, the site of the miracle of the loaves and fishes is now marked by 'the Church of St Peter, very beautiful, though deserted'; and in Cana, scene of the miracle of water into wine, 'there is nothing left there except the monastery'.

He made one interesting reference to the Moslem shrine in Jerusalem, the Haram esh-Sharif, though he does not call it that. In the final phase of the battle for Jerusalem, the Crusaders had pillaged and desecrated the Dome of the Rock and then, though the Mosque of El-Aksa had been surrendered, the Moslem refugees within had been slaughtered, just as the Crusaders had killed the Jews who had taken refuge in their synagogues. With the Crusaders now in power, Christians were

Plaster cast (in Rockefeller Museum) of one of the 'Nazareth capitals', fashioned in France in the 13th century for a basilica in Nazareth
Overleaf: The Georgian and Crusader Monastery of the Cross, Jerusalem

able to visit the Haram esh-Sharif, for the first time in more than four and a half centuries, and the local monks laboured industriously to identify all parts of the site and its structures with events of the Old and New Testaments, without mentioning their later Moslem associations. Thus, when Saewulf inspected the compound, he related its history, beginning with the construction of 'the Temple of Solomon, of wonderful magnitude', and continued with every incident recorded in the Scriptures at which Jesus appeared in the Temple area, from infancy when 'the child Jesus... was offered by His parents with the Virgin Mary, His mother, on the day of her purification'. Only some years after Saewulf's visit would the Dome of the Rock be converted into a church, called Templum Domini (Temple of the Lord), and the Mosque of El-Aksa into the headquarters building of the Crusader Order of Knights Templar (who took their name from the Temple site).

More comprehensive than Saewulf's account is the record of the Russian Abbot Daniel, who reached the country four years later. The conversion of Russians to Christianity had started towards the end of the tenth century and Russian pilgrimage actually began in the eleventh century; but the account of Daniel, prior of a Russian monastery of unknown location, is the earliest record of a Russian pilgrimage to the Holy Land. He arrived in 1106 and spent a year and a half in the country, basing himself at the Pilgrim House in Jerusalem that was maintained by the monks of St Sabba – and occupied at the time by those of them who had escaped the recent massacre at their Judean monastery – and visiting shrines throughout the country under the guidance of one of these knowledgeable survivors.

Like Saewulf, he wrote of the unsettled state of the Latin kingdom in these early years and the danger of pilgrim travel. He, too, had his first taste of danger en route from Jaffa to Jerusalem. (He is the first writer, incidentally, to record that Joppa 'is now known as Jaffa in the language of the Franks'.) He stayed the night not at Ramla but at nearby Lod (Lydda), which had been largely deserted since Suleiman had moved its inhabitants to newly built Ramla in the eighth century, but which the Crusaders were now reviving.

Daniel spent the night there 'in great fear, for the place is deserted, and not far from the town of Ascalon [Ashkelon, which was then still in Moslem hands], whence the Saracens issue and massacre the pilgrims on their way'. Later in his narrative he writes that brigands frequent the road from Jerusalem to Jericho; Saracen bands lie in wait near Solomon's Pools, just south of Bethlehem, for pilgrims journeying to Hebron; travel north to the Sea of Galilee is not possible without an armed escort; and even over the short stretch from Nazareth to Mount Tabor, 'impious Saracens, whose villages are scattered over the mountains and the plain, issue from their homes and massacre travellers on those terrible heights'. Near Beth She'an, 'many lions frequent these parts'.

He offered detailed descriptions of the shrines in the country with which we are

Helmeted Crusader knight, detail of a sculptured corbel from the 13th century Crusader castle of Montfort

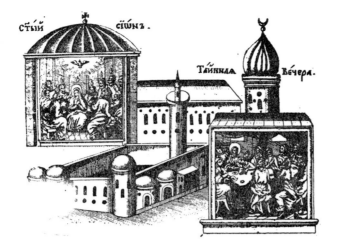

familiar, and he was able to visit those in Samaria and Galilee only because he heard that 'Baldwin, Prince of Jerusalem, was about to make war in the direction of Damascus, and to follow the road to the Sea of Tiberias [Sea of Galilee]'. He therefore 'went to him and, saluting him, said, "I should much like to go with you to the Sea of Tiberias so as to visit all the holy places there. For the love of God take me with you, Prince." The Prince permitted me to follow him with pleasure, and ordered me to join his suite... Thus, then, without fear or peril, we passed those fearful places with the prince's troops; without an escort no one can cross them.'

In his section on the Church of the Holy Sepulchre, the Abbot Daniel has an item on the practice of chipping off pieces of the sepulchre rock for mementoes He writes that after prostrating himself before the tomb, 'I gave the keeper of the keys of the Tomb of the Lord as much as I could, and offered him, according to my means, a small, poor gift. The keeper of the keys, seeing my love for the Holy Sepulchre, pushed back the slab that covers the part of the sacred Tomb on which Christ's head lay, and broke off a morsel of the sacred rock; this he gave me as a blessed memorial, begging me at the same time not to say anything about it in Jerusalem.' To stop this custom and prevent the entire shrine from being carried off piecemeal in the form of souvenirs, the rock was subsequently given a covering of marble. (The Crusader kings did the same with the rock in the Dome of the Rock after they had converted this structure into a church; for this rock also acquired a Christian sanctity and thus became an additional source of mementoes for pilgrims. The authorities accordingly covered it with marble and erected an iron grille round it, which remains to this day.)

We end Daniel's account with his brief but evocative description of the Laura of St Sabba. (A Laura was a small monastic community in a remote and desolate area of the country whose members lived in separate cells fairly near to each other and clustered round the chapel of the community.) The St Sabba Laura was an

The new Basilica of the Annunciation in Nazareth

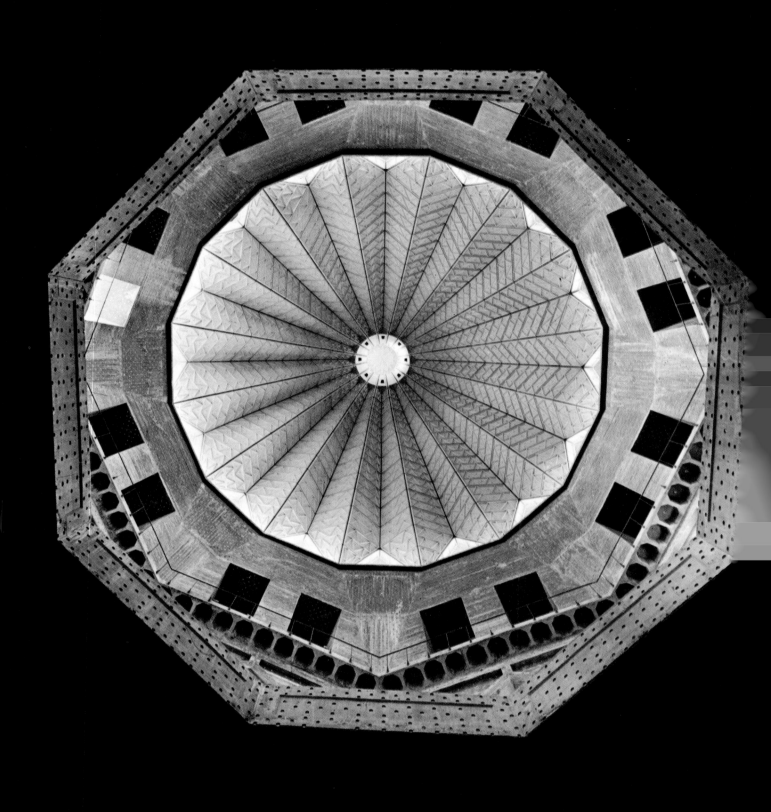

extraordinary group of hermits' cells set sheer against the face of steep rocks in the Judean desert between Bethlehem and the Dead Sea. Today's central structure is the cliffside monastery known as Mar Sabba, and it presents as remarkable a spectacle as it did in Daniel's day or earlier, when the pilgrim Willibald remarked upon it. Daniel writes that its 'situation is a marvellous and indescribable one. A dry torrent bed, terrible to behold, and very deep, is shut in by high walls of rock, to which the cells are fixed and kept in place by the hand of God in a surprising and fearful manner. These cells, fastened to the precipices flanking this frightful torrent, are attached to the rocks like the stars to the firmament. There are three churches in the midst of the cells… The place, situated in the midst of rocky mountains, is arid; all the country round is parched for want of water, and the hermits dwelling there have nothing but rain-water.'

In the course of the next few decades, pilgrimage mounted, and in the great ports of Europe, embarkation points for the Holy Land, the pilgrims assembled, most of them dressed in grey cowl and broad-brimmed hat, a staff in one hand and a sack over a shoulder, and all bearing a red cross on their backs. Many wore long beards and hair unshorn, and some walked barefoot.

To guide them on their pilgrimage, several short works appeared at this time, most of them anonymous, pointing out and describing the holy sites that should be visited, rather like impersonal guide-books. These differ from the pilgrim narratives mentioned so far which are more in the nature of personal journals; but in later journals, we find several authors using exactly the same words in some of their descriptions – probably of those places and objects which they did not themselves observe – suggesting their use of a common source. One of the best known contemporary source-guides was an 1130 work ascribed to one Fetellus; and two well-known pilgrim records of some forty years later which use Fetellus and some other compendium as a common reference text are those of John of Wurzburg (1160-1170) and Theoderich (1172).

Fetellus was a prelate of Antioch, and his name is associated with the anonymous treatise because his edition of it was for long the one most widely used. Though much of the text is taken up with scriptural history and geography, it yields some items new to us. By now, thirty years after the Crusader conquest, Jerusalem abounds with new churches, monasteries and hospices. The Church of the Holy Sepulchre was undergoing reconstruction – 'a large church is building' and construction was going on over 'the place where the blessed Helena found the Holy Cross'. The Haram esh-Sharif area had been given over to the recently established Order of Knights Templar: 'Below the site of the Temple is the dwelling of the new soldiers who guard Jerusalem.' This 'dwelling' was the Mosque of El-Aksa. The Templars had carried out certain alterations, building an armoury on its west side, later a church on its east side, and stabling their horses in the vaulted substructures beneath. (These soon became known as 'Solomon's Stables', for the site was the traditional location of the palace of king Solomon, but they are in fact the work of Herod.) No structural changes were made to the Dome of the Rock after it was converted into a church.

An interesting Fetellus reference to another site in Jerusalem relates to Herod's palace, the Citadel, inside Jaffa Gate: 'The tower which is now called that of David was built by Herod.' This is one of the few early documents which give the correct origin of the popularly termed 'Tower of David'.

In Bethlehem, the description of the Church of the Nativity, 'built of considerable beauty', includes a reference to familiar fourth century pilgrims who have themselves become objects of pilgrimage interest. Upon leaving the crypt of the manger, one proceeded through the caverns and 'finds near the door two crypts, one higher, the other lower. In the higher lies the most blessed Paula, at whose feet lies her daughter, viz., the most sacred Virgin Eustochium. One descends to the lower crypt by many steps, and there is the sepulchre in which lies the most sacred body of the most blessed Jerome, the renowned Doctor.'

John of Wurzburg, a patriotic German priest – he thought it was an injustice to the German Crusaders to attribute the recovery of the Holy Land to the French alone – made the pilgrimage between the years 1160 and 1170. He called Jerusalem 'the glorious metropolis of Judea' and, 'according to philosophers, [it] is placed in the middle of the world'. This was a popular belief in medieval times, and there are many contemporary maps which show the city as the world's geographical centre.

Inside the Dome of the Rock, by now very much the Temple Church, John of Wurzburg recorded the numerous inscriptions on walls and columns of verses relating to New Testament incidents at the Jewish Temple in which Jesus figured. He also mentioned 'a stone, which is treated with great veneration... it having been trodden on and bearing the mark of the Lord's foot'. (When the Moslems recaptured Jerusalem, the Christian 'Mark of the Lord's Foot' was shown as the 'Footprint of Mohammed' – and it still is.) He had this observation on the Moslem reaction to the use now made of their building: 'The figure of the Holy Cross has been placed by the Christians [on the top of the dome], which is very offensive to the Saracens, and many of them would be willing to expend much gold to have it taken away.'

In the east wall of the Temple compound, which was (and is still) the east wall of the city, is 'the Golden Gate, through which our Lord on the fifth day before His passion rode in triumph... and was greeted with palm branches...', and John of Wurzburg adds that this gate 'is never opened to anyone except on Palm Sunday'. This magnificent double-arched Golden Gate which our pilgrim saw was a Byzantine structure which stands to this day. It is associated with the traditions of all three faiths. An early Jewish tradition holds that it is through this gate

that the Messiah will enter Jerusalem. For Christians it was the way Jesus came into Jerusalem. Moslems held that this was the gate of judgement referred to in the Koran (Surah 57, verse 13), 'the inner side whereof containeth mercy, while the outer side thereof is toward the doom'. Though it may still be entered from the Temple compound, the Golden Gate is now blocked from the outside, having been sealed by the Moslems (scholars differ as to whether it was in the twelfth or the sixteenth century) almost certainly for security reasons. But it is a Moslem belief that it was really done to prevent the entry of the liberating Jewish Messiah, and also to ensure that the gate would have no 'outer side... toward the doom' on Judgement Day.

John of Wurzburg then writes that at the southern end of the Temple compound 'is the palace which Solomon is said to have built' – site of the Mosque of El-Aksa, which he does not mention by name – 'wherein is a wondrous stable of such size that it is able to contain more than two thousand horses or fifteen hundred camels. Close to this palace the Knights Templar have many spacious and connected buildings, and also the foundations of a new and large church which is not yet finished.' (The foundations of the apse of this Crusader church are visible today on the east side of the mosque.)

Theoderich has a better description of 'Solomon's Stable', calling it, correctly, 'a wondrous and intricate building resting on piers and containing an endless complication of arches and vaults'. Incidentally, both accept the popular assumption that it was built by king Solomon when he constructed his palace on this site. Though it was being used by the Crusaders to stable their horses when our pilgrims saw it, Herod had built it not for this purpose at all but simply as part of the substructures to support the Temple platform. It is extremely well-preserved and looks the same today as it did when Herod's workmen finished it towards the end of the first century BC.

The reconstruction of the Church of the Holy Sepulchre was completed when John of Wurzburg and Theoderich visited Jerusalem, and what they saw was a single large structure, as today, integrating all the sacred sites associated with the Crucifixion. Theoderich was the first writer to report on the Chapel of the Invention of the Cross in addition to the Chapel of Helena, both of which may be seen today: 'One goes down thirty steps and more to the venerable Chapel of St Helena the empress... Hence again... one descends fifteen or rather more steps into a subterranean cave, where ...the empress is said to have discovered the cross of our Lord.' Thus, the tradition of the finding of the cross and Helena as finder is as strong as ever.

The birthplace of John the Baptist is referred to by Theoderich, who writes of the Jerusalem suburb known as Ein Karem and of the two occasions recorded in the New Testament which were believed to have been associated with it and which were commemorated by two churches. One marks the place where Mary, mother of Jesus, met Zacharias and Elizabeth, parents of John the Baptist, and the other the traditional site where John was born.

This pilgrim also reports on the Church of the Holy Cross, which is mentioned by earlier pilgrims, located in what became known as the Valley of the Cross (just below today's new Israel Museum), on the site where 'stood the trunk of the tree from which was cut the cross whereon the Saviour hung for our salvation. This church... is strongly fortified with towers, walls, and battlements, against the treacherous attacks of the infidels; it is moreover adorned with houses, dining-rooms, chambers, and dwellings of all kinds...' Today's Monastery of the Cross looks indeed like a medieval fortress, and it contains a small and beautifully preserved Crusader church.

This site was also visited and described by Iohannes Phocas, Greek monk, ex-soldier of the Byzantine emperor, and native of Crete, who was the last pilgrim to leave a record of the Crusader Kingdom of Jerusalem, reaching Palestine in 1185, two years before the Moslem reconquest of the city. He entered the country from the north and his first stop was Acre, now a thriving and cosmopolitan Mediterranean port. It was 'a large city, and so populous as to surpass all the rest. It receives all the merchant ships, and thither all pilgrims for Christ's sake by sea and land betake themselves.' But in those days, too, urban expansion exacted its price and its problems, however different from those of today, for Phocas added: 'Here, the air being corrupted by the enormous influx of strangers, various diseases arise, and lead to frequent deaths among them, the consequence of which is evil smells and corruption of the air, and the misfortune of this city is beyond remedy.'

Like the Abbot Daniel, he had some interesting words on the monastic centres. After writing of the Monastery of St Sabba, he told of another well-known monastery which offers as dramatic a sight today as it did then. This is the Monastery of Deir el-Kelt, in the wadi Kelt, a ravine between Jerusalem and Jericho, and, like Mar Sabba, it clings to the face of a precipice. Phocas says it is 'a thing not to be believed when described, and inspiring wonder when beheld; for the cells of the monks are the mouths of caves, and the church itself and the cemetery is excavated out of the solid rock, and is heated to a [great] degree by the rays of the sun... It was with some danger that I climbed into and out of this monastery, both because of the precipitous nature of the place, and the overpowering heat...'

He added that the countryside near wadi Kelt 'abounds with springs of water' – there is a magnificent one there today, with an adjoining pool (in which one may bathe) which is icy even on the hottest summer day – 'for the use of the monasteries which have been founded in the wilderness; for the land, having been divided and parcelled out among these holy monasteries, has become well wooded and full of vines; so that the monks have built towers upon their fields, and reap rich harvests from them.'

Some of these lands would soon be lost – with the loss of Crusader Jerusalem.

The cliff-hanging Monastery of Deir el-Kelt is perched above a ravine between Jerusalem and Jericho

7 BENJAMIN OF TUDELA

In the early days of the Crusader Kingdom of Jerusalem, the treatment of Jews was harsh and the ban on their entry into Jerusalem was strictly enforced. By the middle of the twelfth century, however, with a weakened Crusader authority more lax, there was some easing of anti-Jewish restrictions and a few Jewish families were allowed to settle in the capital, apparently because of their needed skills, notably dyeing. At the same time, some prominent overseas Jews were permitted to make the pilgrimage. Among them was a scholarly Spanish Jew named Benjamin, from the northern town of Tudela near the Pyrenees. He was one of the great travellers of the Middle Ages, and the classic account of his journeyings sheds much light on the life and look of the countries of the Near and Middle East in those days.

Like the Christian and Moslem travellers, he is much concerned with his own people; but unlike most of his counterparts of other faiths, he does not confine his descriptions to shrines alone. He is also deeply interested in the human condition of his fellow Jews, and he makes a point of visiting places in the Diaspora where there is a Jewish community and giving details of its size, the vocations of its members – and even the names of its elders. Thus, when he gets to coastal Tyre, on the threshold of northern Palestine, he gives a good, brief account of the city, and then adds: 'The Jews of Tyre are ship-owners and manufacturers of the celebrated Tyrian glass: the purple dye is also found in this vicinity... About four hundred Jews reside here, the principal of whom are the judge Reb Ephraim Mitsri, Reb Meir of Carcasson...'

Benjamin of Tudela left northern Spain in 1159 and proceeded through Italy and Greece to Constantinople, thence to the Greek islands, to Antioch, through Syria, and down to Palestine, where he made a lengthy sojourn. From there he went to Baghdad and Persia, returning via Arabia to Egypt, then Sicily, on to Germany and so home. In the centuries that followed, his work was translated into all the major vernacular languages of Europe, and used as a standard reference by scholars on the situation in these countries in the twelfth century.

The focal point of his travel-narrative is Palestine, where he arrived in the year

Samaritans hold aloft a text of the Samaritan Bible at the Succot Festival
celebrated by their sect on Mount Gerizim

1167, entering it from the north at Acre. 'It is the frontier town of Palestine; and, in consequence of its situation on the shore of the Mediterranean and of its large port, it is the principal place of disembarkation of all pilgrims who come by sea to visit Jerusalem. There are here about two hundred Jewish inhabitants...' From there he moved down to Haifa, 'overlooked by Mount Carmel. Under the mountain are many Jewish sepulchres, and near the summit is the cavern of Elijah.' This was the area where the Prophet Elijah challenged the prophets of Baal in the ninth century BC days of king Ahab and queen Jezebel (1 Kings XVIII), and the 'Cave of Elijah', where he is believed to have taken refuge on one of his frequent flights from the anger of the queen, is still revered as a sacred Jewish shrine. It is holy also to Christians and Moslems.

Benjamin continued south to Caesarea, 'very elegant and beautiful', and then cut inland, 'to Sebaste. This is the ancient Shomron [Samaria], where you may still trace the site of the palace of Ahab, king of Israel.' Little remains of that palace today, but at archaeological excavations carried out in 1932, parts of the lower courses were discovered of the walls of the citadel built by Ahab's father Omri, who established the city.

Benjamin then visited nearby Nablus, biblical Shechem, where he met the community of 'Cutheans. These are Samaritan Jews, commonly called Samaritans... who observe the Mosaic law only', and not the Talmud, the body of oral law which governs Judaism. He then described their worship 'on Mount Gerizim', one of the two mounts overlooking Nablus which is still the main centre of the Samaritan community. Benjamin added that 'on Passover they offer burnt-offerings on the altar which they have erected on Mount Gerizim from the stones put up by the Children of Israel after they had crossed the Jordan. They pretend to be of the tribe of Ephraim...' The Samaritans still conduct their Passover ceremony in the same dramatic way, roasting the paschal lamb over a fire at night on the summit of Mount Gerizim.

From Samaria, Benjamin travelled south to Jerusalem, and whatever his emotions on entering the holy city, the record in his diary shows the sober restraint of the clinical reporter. He found it 'a small city strongly fortified with three walls. It contains a numerous population, composed of Jacobites, Armenians, Greeks, Georgians, Franks'—the different Christian sects in the city—'and indeed of people of all tongues.' He then mentioned the Jewish community: 'The dyeing-house is rented by the year, and the exclusive privilege of dyeing is purchased from the king by the Jews of Jerusalem, two hundred of whom dwell in one corner of the city, under the tower of David', that is, close to Jaffa Gate, near today's Armenian Quarter.

He tells us something of the Crusader knights and their army system. The Hospitalers have a hospice which supports 'four hundred knights, and affords shelter to the sick'. There is a second, on the Temple Mount – he is referring to the Mosque

Restored Crusader courtyard of the convent and pilgrims' hospital, which are now part of the Lutheran compound near the Church of the Holy Sepulchre

Left: An early photograph of the Western Wall

Right: Jewish cemetery (foreground) on the Mount of Olives. Photo taken after the Six Day War, showing desecration of the graves before the war

of El-Aksa – which is called 'the hospice of Solomon, being the palace originally built by king Solomon. This also harbours and furnishes four hundred knights [the Templars], who are ever ready to wage war, over and above those knights who arrive from the country of the Franks and other parts of Christendom. These generally have taken a vow upon themselves to stay a year or two, and they remain until the period of their vow is expired.' The comparatively few knights of the Templar and Hospitaler Orders served as a kind of standing army and they were periodically reinforced by volunteers from Europe who did one or two years of military service in Palestine. Their numbers were meagre and clearly insufficient to hold out for long against the rising Moslem tide, particularly as immigration from the west had greatly declined, and from the few words of Benjamin we get a clue as to why the kingdom of Jerusalem was to go under when it faced its crucial test against an energetic Moslem leader twenty years later.

Benjamin mentioned, but did not describe, 'the large place of worship' of the Crusaders, called 'the Sepulchre', adding that it 'is visited by all pilgrims'. He also referred to the Dome of the Rock, standing 'opposite the place of the holy Temple, which is occupied at present by [a church] called Templum Domini... In front of it you see the Western Wall, one of the walls which formed the... ancient Temple... and all Jews resort thither to say their prayers near the wall of the courtyard.'

In the 'valley of Jehoshaphat', which is really a section of the Kidron valley, 'you may see the pillar erected on Absalom's place'. This is the cone-topped rock sculptured in the form of a small temple which is known as the Pillar of Absalom to this day, but which is really a second century BC Jewish tomb and has no historical association with the son of David. He also mentioned 'the great spring of Shiloah [Siloam]'. At the end of the eighth century BC, king Hezekiah tunnelled a water conduit through the rock from the Gihon spring to the pool of Siloam (II Kings XX, 20), but all Benjamin of Tudela saw was the spring and the pool. Not until seven centuries later, in 1880, was the biblical record confirmed, with the chance discovery of the tunnel in a perfect state of preservation. Midway along the tunnel, inscribed on a stone plaque on the wall in classical Hebrew prose, was an account of how the tunnel had been excavated by two teams of miners starting at opposite ends, working towards each other and meeting in the middle.

Our medieval traveller next went up to the summit of the Mount of Olives and described what he saw of the surrounding countryside, also recalling its biblical background. At his feet, on the slopes of the mount, he noted the ancient Jewish cemetery; and he added: 'Some of the sepulchres had stones with inscriptions upon them, but the Christians destroy these monuments, and use the stones in building their houses!' This, we must recall, was in the twelfth century, but it has a familiar ring in the twentieth. In 1949, Israel's War of Independence ended with a divided city of Jerusalem, the half which included the Mount of Olives falling under the

Top: The tomb of Rachel, near the entrance to Bethlehem, during the 18th century
Bottom: The same, at beginning of this century

control of the Hashemite Kingdom of Jordan and barred to Jews. Only with the Six Day War in June 1967 was the city reunited, under Israel administration, and the Jews were able to inspect their old cemetery. They found that in the course of the previous eighteen and a half years of Moslem rule, the cemetery had been desecrated, the tombstones left on the site had been battered, and the rest had been removed by the Moslems for use as building materials. Some of them were found, still with their Hebrew inscriptions, as paving stones, and on the floors of bathrooms and lavatories in the buildings of a nearby camp that had been constructed for officers of the Jordan Arab Legion.

On the road from Jerusalem to Bethlehem, and just before reaching that city, Benjamin saw 'the monument which points out the grave of Rachel', wife of the Patriarch Jacob and mother of Joseph and Benjamin, who died young 'and was buried on the way to Ephrath, which is Bethlehem'. (Genesis XXXV, 19.) The tomb 'is covered by a cupola, which rests upon four pillars'. (It has undergone structural alterations since then, but it is still revered as a Jewish shrine, and Moslems, too, hold it sacred.) From Bethlehem he continued southward to Hebron, and he reported a curious form of extortion practised upon Jewish visitors in 'the field of Machpelah' – the Cave of the Patriarchs. 'Here is the large place of worship called St Abraham, which during the time of the Mohammedans was a synagogue. The Gentiles have erected six sepulchres in this place, which they pretend to be those of [the Patriarchs]; the pilgrims are told that they are the sepulchres of the fathers, and money is extorted from them. But if any Jew come, who gives an additional fee to the keeper of the cave, an iron door is opened... and, with a burning candle in his hands, the visitor descends into a first cave, which is empty, traverses a second in the same state, and at last reaches a third, which contains six sepulchres, those of Abraham, Isaac and Jacob, and of Sarah, Rebecca and Leah, one opposite the other.'

Of Ashkelon, Benjamin said that 'this city is very large and handsome; and merchants from all parts resort to it, on account of its convenient situation on the confines of Egypt.'

Travelling north to Galilee, Benjamin visited Tiberias, with its 'hot waters which spout forth from under ground', and its 'warm baths. In the vicinity is the synagogue' – two ancient synagogues there have recently been excavated – and 'numerous Jewish sepulchres', which he lists. From there he went to Meron, near Safad, of much interest to Jews to this day because 'in a cave near this place are the tombs of Hillel and Shamai', the first century BC Jewish sages, talmudic giants who founded schools of thought which had a massive impact on Judaic scholarship. (In the sixteenth century, Meron became a kindred centre with Safad of the Cabbalists, the esoteric group of pious scholars whose study was Jewish mysticism.)

Galilee was the last stop in Palestine for Benjamin of Tudela. From there he took the road to Damascus.

Façade of synagogue in Safad where 'Ha'Ari', Rabbi Isaac Lurie, the 16th century Cabbalah sage, used to pray

במהרא המקום הזה
זהב יעקב מרן האר״זל
בשנת המקדש תער״א

8 THE SARACEN CONQUEST

The Crusaders lost their Kingdom of Jerusalem in 1187 with the defeat of their armies at the decisive battle of the Horns of Hattin, suffered at the hands of the brilliant Salah ad-Din, known to the western world as Saladin. An Armenian Kurd by nationality and a Moslem by faith, Saladin (1138-1193) had absorbed the best traditions of Moslem culture in Damascus, the main centre of Moslem learning, where his father, Ayyub, was governor, and where he was educated. Saladin himself became governor of Egypt in his early thirties. By 1185, he had also gained control of Syria and northern Iraq by battle and diplomacy, so that he was now master of all the territories surrounding the Crusader kingdom. Two years later, he crossed into Lower Galilee, established himself at Tiberias, lured the Crusader armies into battle at the Horns of Hattin where the advantages were entirely with him, and took a heavy toll of their forces, capturing many of them, including their king. Within weeks, most of the Crusader positions in the rest of the country, among them Jerusalem, capitulated.

The chivalrous Saladin behaved gently and generously with the Christian inhabitants of Jerusalem, sparing their lives and their churches – in contrast to the actions of the Crusaders when they had captured the city eighty-eight years earlier. He resumed possession of the Temple Mount, cleared the Haram esh-Sharif of all marks of Christianity and re-dedicated it. Inside the Dome of the Rock, the plaster with which the Crusaders had covered the Koranic inscriptions and which now bore Christian inscriptions was removed, and both this building and the Mosque of El-Aksa were purified with rose water and restored to their former state.

The collapse of the Crusader kingdom shocked Christian Europe and prompted the Third Crusade, an Anglo-French force led by king Philip Augustus of France and king Richard the Lion-Heart of England, and since they commanded navies which Saladin lacked, they were able to recapture the port of Acre in 1191 and establish a stronghold in the north. In the course of the following year king Richard managed to gain control of the coastal strip as far south as Jaffa, and also reconquer a short inland belt from Jaffa to Ramla and Lod. But he failed to re-take Jerusalem, and in September 1192 he signed a treaty with Saladin, based on the *status quo*.

An Ottoman 'Firman' (certificate of recognition), granted to the Armenian community in 1520

The Crusaders would retain the stretch of coastline they held; Christians would be free to visit their holy places in Jerusalem; and Moslems and Christians would be allowed to pass through each other's lands. With the armistice signed, Richard returned to Europe with his men, and Saladin to Damascus, where he died the following spring. For all its sanctity, Jerusalem, to Moslem Saladin, was no more than an unimportant provincial city. Acre became the Crusaders' headquarters town.

In the three decades which followed Saladin's death, the Moslem unity which he had fashioned fell apart, and in 1229, the renowned emperor Frederik II of Germany was able to negotiate a treaty with the sultan of Egypt (who was in conflict with the sultan in Damascus) whereby Jerusalem was restored to the Crusaders, and they also received Bethlehem, Nazareth and other places, a strip of territory linking Jerusalem with the coast, and permission to refortify Jaffa and Caesarea. (These later refortifications of Caesarea, carried out mostly by Louis IX of France in about 1250, were recently excavated and restored, and are the most extensive Crusader remains in Israel today.) The Moslems retained the Dome of the Rock and the Mosque of El-Aksa in Jerusalem.

This situation lasted until 1244, with a gap in 1239 when an army from Damascus captured Jerusalem, but were thrown out a year later. However, in 1244, an army of Khwarizmian Turks, momentarily allied to the Egyptian sultan, took Jerusalem and sacked it.

From now on, the Crusaders were again confined to a small stretch of territory along the coastal belt and in the north, and were again headquartered at Acre. But this truncated 'Kingdom of Acre' was soon to be whittled down even further by new forces which had seized power in Egypt in 1250. These were the Mamelukes. (The Mamelukes were manumitted soldier-slaves – *mamluk* was the common Arabic term for a freed slave – who had been acquired in the slave-markets as children by the Moslem caliphs, and trained as warriors to make up for the military inadequacies of the caliphs' subjects. They were mostly Turks and Circassians from Russia, the Caucasus and central Asia. Saladin and his dynastic successors had also used them as their vanguard troops to battle the Crusaders. They had now overthrown their former masters and become a military ruling caste, and they would control the region, including Palestine, for the next 267 years.)

It was notably after the accession of the Mameluke sultan Baybars, in 1260, that the Crusaders were squeezed into a smaller and smaller enclave. The pressure was maintained by Baybars' successors, and in May 1291, the defences of Acre, the last Crusader stronghold, were overcome. The surviving Crusaders took ship for Cyprus. Thus ended Crusader rule on Palestine soil. The Mamelukes then systematically destroyed all Crusader fortifications.

There are several anonymous pilgrim records covering different sections of this period. They are of uneven standard, and most of them yield few new facts, concentrating largely on the scriptural history of each site that is mentioned. One,

Detail of a 1770 painting in the Monastery of the Cross depicting pilgrim sites in and around Jerusalem

however, transmits the 'feel' of the country after Saladin's conquest and offers the best view of medieval Jerusalem before the return of the city to the Crusaders. This lively tract, called *La Citez de Jherusalem* (The City of Jerusalem), was written in about the year 1220, and the unknown pilgrim describes its markets as well as its churches, streets, gates, walls and ceremonies. 'The great road which goes from the Tower of David straight to the Golden Gate is called David Street.' (It still is.) 'On the left hand is a large Place where they sell corn. A little farther down this David Street one comes to a street on the left hand which is called Patriarch Street, because the Patriarch dwells at the top of it. There is a door on the right hand... by which one enters into the Church of the Sepulchre.' This area round the most sacred Christian place (today's Christian Quarter) lies in the northwestern corner of the city, and it was here that the pilgrims concentrated.

Running off David Street, about half-way down, 'is a covered street, vaulted over, called the Street of Herbs, where they sell all the herbs, and all the fruits of the city, and spices'. (This street still retains its twelfth century vaulting.) 'At the top of this street there is a place where they sell fish. And behind the market where they sell the fish, is a very large Place on the left hand where cheese, chickens, and eggs are sold. On the right hand of this Market are the shops of the Syrian gold-workers... Close to the Street of Herbs is a street called Mal-quisinat ('Bad-Cooking'). In this street they cooked food for the pilgrims, and sold it, and they washed their heads. And they went from this street to the Sepulchre. In front of this Mal-quisinat street there is a street called the Covered Street, where they sell stuffs: it is entirely vaulted over. And one goes by this street to the Sepulchre.' The three roofed alleys mentioned by our unknown pilgrim guide, Mal-quisinat, the Street of Herbs and the Covered Street, still remain, and curiously enough, at their northern end there are today a cluster of barber-shops, as there were in those days, where they 'washed the heads' of the pilgrims and shaved them before they entered the Holy Sepulchre.

Just beyond the start of Temple Street (the continuation of David Street), 'you come to Butchers' Place, where they sell the meat of the town. On the right hand there is another street, by which one goes to the German hospital, which is called Germans' Street.' This was the area where the third Crusader Order, the Teutonic Knights, were headquartered. It lies in the southeastern section of the city, which later became known as the 'Jewish Quarter'.

(There have recently been some dramatic archaeological finds in this Quarter. An expedition headed by the Hebrew University's Professor Nahman Avigad which carried out a three months' excavation at the end of 1969 revealed that it was first settled in the seventh century BC during the closing period of the Judean monarchy. [As we write, the excavations are being resumed and extended northwards.] The professor said that 'by great good fortune', the Crusaders who had built on this site some eight hundred years ago had left enough of the earlier structures standing to make possible a reconstruction of the ancient settlement. The dig uncovered a plastered floor and a plastered pit, probably part of an olive press, containing vessels found *in situ* which definitely belonged to the seventh century BC. At this archaeological stratum there was a layer of red earth on which the Jews had built their first houses. This discovery shows that Jewish Jerusalem first spread to this western hillock when the First Temple was still standing.

Another dramatic find were two fragments of wall plaster, belonging to the Second Temple period, bearing the decoration of a seven-branched candelabrum. Executed at a time when this type of candelabrum was one of the ritual vessels in the Temple, it is probably the authentic representation, and more accurate in detail than the one depicted in the Arch of Titus in Rome. These fragments, together with other portions of fresco found by the archaeologists, are believed to have decorated a wall of a Herodian public building. [The seven-branched candelabrum is the emblem of the State of Israel.] The excavations brought to light nine levels of occupation, from the Israelite to the Crusader period.)

Jewish pilgrims and settlers began arriving in Jerusalem soon after Saladin's victory and his easing of the Crusader restrictions against them. The records show that they started to return in 1190 and within a short time there was again a Jewish community in the holy city. They were visited by Rabbi Samuel ben Samson and several companions who made the pilgrimage in 1210. He records in his *Itinerary* that 'we arrived at Jerusalem by the western end of the city, rending our garments on beholding it, as it has been ordained we should do' – a sign of mourning for the destruction of the Temple. 'It was a moment of tenderest emotion, and we wept bitterly... We entered by the [western] gate...' Access to the Temple Mount itself was now apparently permitted, for Rabbi Samuel writes that 'on the Sabbath day we recited the Afternoon Prayer on the spot where the uncircumcised [Gentiles] had time and again set up a sanctuary... The Ishmaelites [Arabs] venerate this spot. Only the foundations [of the Temple] remain now in existence, but the place where the Ark stood is still to be seen.' Movement seems to have been free, for he and his companions, after leaving Jerusalem, visited several other Old Testament sites in the country.

One year later, in 1211, three hundred rabbis and scholars from France and England came to settle and they greatly enriched the cultural life of the community. But two decades later, with the return of the Crusaders to Jerusalem, Jews of the city were again subject to much suffering – and they suffered further when the Crusaders were driven out and the city sacked in 1244. In 1267, there arrived in the country the renowned Jewish scholar from Gerona in Spain, Rabbi Moshe ben Nahman, better known as the Ramban or as Nahmanides, and he found a minute and impoverished community in a desolated Jerusalem. As he wrote in letters to his sons, there had been a massacre of Jews in the city seven years earlier, though some had

Episodes in the pilgrimage of a 15th century monk as depicted in a contemporary illuminated manuscript

managed to escape to Shechem, in Samaria, carrying with them their Scrolls of the Law (the Torah). Though Jerusalem was now a ravaged city, the few Jews who lived there enjoyed freedom of worship, and Rabbi Moshe remained to revive the congregation, reconstructing a synagogue and a centre of talmudic study, and, as he writes, 'we have sent to the city of Shechem to bring back from there the Torah Scrolls which were in Jerusalem and which were taken there when the vandals came, and now they will be placed in our synagogue and there we shall pray...' The synagogue bore the name of the Ramban ever since. Praying there were not only members of the local congregation but also numerous Jewish pilgrims, for whenever there was a lull in the fighting and movement was possible, there was a resumption of pilgrimage. As the Ramban records in his letters, 'many come to Jerusalem, men and women from Damascus' – and other parts of the Diaspora – 'to see the place of the Temple and to mourn over its destruction. And he who has been privileged to see Jerusalem in its ruin will be privileged to see it restored to its glory...' The Ramban's own pilgrimage, wrote one of his disciples, did much to stimulate further Jewish pilgrimage and settlement in the years that followed.

The roiling jealousies and quarrels between the various Christian sects, notably during the second half of the Crusader period, and their mutual mistrust and contempt are recorded in extraordinarily pungent language by the French Prelate Jacques de Vitry, writing between about the year 1226 and his death in 1240. Born at a time when the Christian world was dazed by Saladin's conquest of Jerusalem, and brought up on Crusader memory, de Vitry became a passionate Crusader, preaching and fighting for the restoration of the Latin kingdom. He eventually became bishop of Acre, papal legate in France and Germany, witnessed the brief return of Jerusalem to Christendom through the emperor Frederick, and was appointed patriarch of Jerusalem in 1240, but died before he could take office.

De Vitry added a dimension to pilgrim records by giving us a glimpse into the character and passions of the diverse components of the Christian community; and no thirteenth century writer better transmits the feeling of the Crusader epoch. Assuredly he is partisan; but his trenchant record enables us better to understand why the Crusades ultimately ended in total defeat.

He tells us first of his own people, Crusaders and support personnel from the west, and the virtues and failings of the varied national contingents. Across the seas to the Holy Land came 'they of Genoa, Venice, and Pisa. Thither came the strength of the nations, especially from France and Germany, men of war. The former are more powerful at sea, the latter on land; the one are fitter for seafights, and better able to do battle on the water by their practice and use thereof; the latter are better soldiers on land, well skilled in the wars, and stouter warriors on horseback with sword and lance; the glory of the former is in their galleys, of the latter in their horses.

Crosses marked by pilgrims on a pillar in the Church of the Holy Sepulchre

'The Italians are graver and more discreet, prudent and wary, frugal in eating, sober in drinking. They make long and polished speeches, are wise in their counsels, eager and zealous to further the interests of their own states, grasping and provident for the future, unwilling to serve under others... They are very necessary to the Holy Land, not only for fighting, but for seafaring, and carrying merchandise, pilgrims, and victuals. As they are sparing of food and drink, they live longer in the East than other nations of the West.

'The Germans, French, Bretons, English, and others from beyond the Alps, are less wary, and more reckless, less careful in their dealings, more prodigal in eating and drinking, more profuse in expense, less cautious in words, rasher and less prudent in their plans... Because of their levity and intemperance, they are called fools by the Pullani.' Pullani is his term for native-born Christians of Crusader fathers and indigenous mothers, for while most surviving Crusaders would return to Europe after a campaign, a number remained and married local women.

De Vitry deals kindly with such men, for he cannot think harshly of anyone who joined a Crusade and fought; and this prompts him to offer a rare word of praise for the various local Christian sects whose daughters have married Crusaders: 'In the Holy Land there are many other [Christian] nations, with different customs, who differ greatly from one another in their Divine service and religious rites, to wit, Syrians, Greeks, Jacobites, Maronites, Nestorians, Armenians and Georgians who both for trade, agriculture, and other useful arts, are very necessary to the Holy Land, that they may sow the land, and plant vineyards...'

However, later in his account, he attacked 'the Greeks and the Syrians' who 'lamentably misunderstand the Creed'; the Jacobites who... 'have for a long time wandered in lamentable darkness and error'; the Nestorians whose founder 'infected most of the East with the deadly poison of his doctrine'; and he was equally scathing about the Maronites, whose founder was 'a heretic'. The Armenians and the Georgians were let off more lightly, though he was very critical of their theology and their rites.

Most members of these sects had long been established in the land and lived in mixed settlements with the Moslems, and this, plus their heresy, prompts him to forget his earlier patronage, so that he says of the Syrian Christians: 'They are... helpless as women in battle... They are for the most part untrustworthy, double-dealers, cunning foxes even as the Greeks, liars and turncoats, lovers of success, easily won over by bribes, men who say one thing and mean another, who think nothing of theft and robbery. For a small sum of money they become spies and tell the secrets of the Christians to the Saracens'.

De Vitry's greatest contempt and anger is reserved for the locally born sons of expatriate Crusaders. They are 'an evil and perverse generation, wicked and degenerate sons, corrupt men, who proceeded from the aforesaid pilgrims, religious men, acceptable to God and full of grace, even as lees from wine, dregs from

12th century illustrated pilgrimage itinerary from the main cities of Europe to the Holy Land
Overleaf: Vaulted bazaar in the Old City of Jerusalem

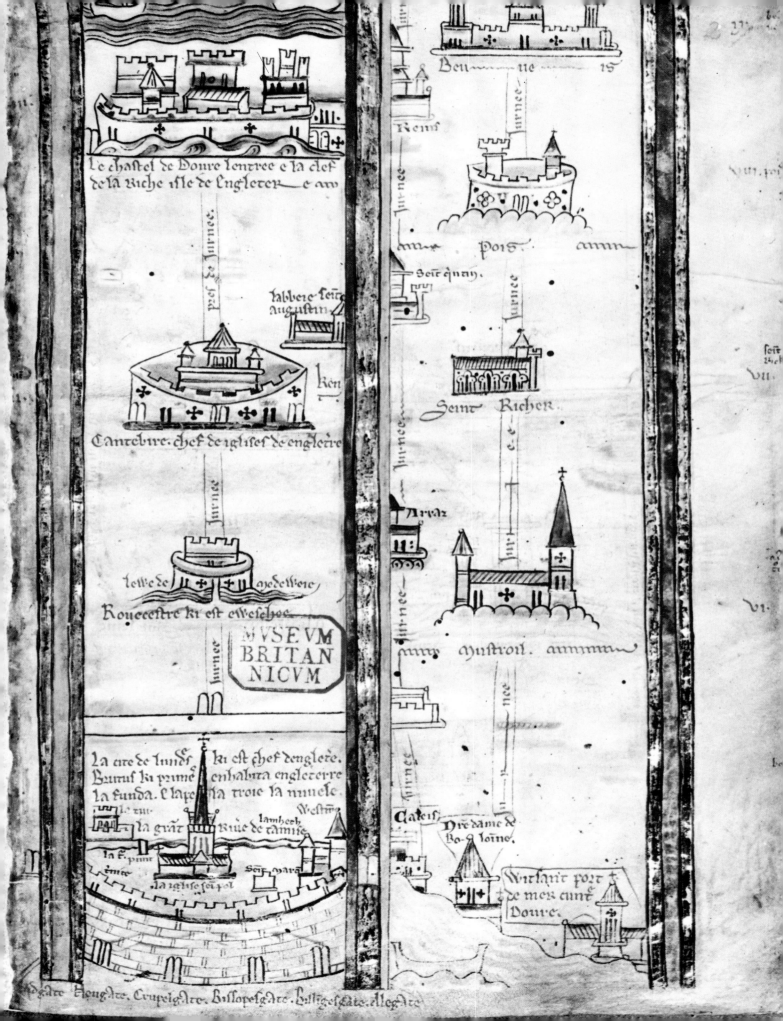

Le chastel de Doure lentree e la clef
de la riche isle de Engleter · e au

labbeie seint
augustin

Ken

Cantebire · chef de iglises de engletere

Jurnee

Tour de londe · Roecestre

Rouecestre ki est eveskee

MVSEVM
BRITAN
NICVM

La cire de lundes · ki est chef denglete.
Brutus ki prime enhabita engleterre
la funda · e lapela troie la nuuele

Westm̄

lambeth

la grāt riue de tamise

la iglise sei pol

Seit marti

Beu̅̅̅̅ne   15

Reins   Jurnee

Jurnee

Jurnee

Jurnee   pois

Seit ҫ́nay

Jurnee

Seint Richer

Jurnee

Aƚaƚ

Jurnee

Jurnee

Jurnee   Mustroil

Jurnee

Jurnee

Cales   Jurnee

N̄re dame de
Bo-g loine

Witsaut port
de mer cunt
Doure

olives, tares from wheat, and rust from silver; they succeeded to their fathers' property but not to their good morals; they squandered the wordly wealth which their fathers had won by the shedding of their own blood, fighting manfully against the infidels for the honour of God. Their children, who are called Pullani, were brought up in luxury, soft and effeminate, more used to baths than battles, addicted to unclean and riotous living, clad like women in soft robes... how slow and slothful, how timid and cowardly... They make treaties with the Saracens, and are glad to be at peace with Christ's enemies... Now the pilgrims who come with very great toil and at ruinous expense from far away, out of devotion and help to them... are not only treated with ingratitude by these Pullani, but they make themselves offensive to them in divers ways... When by their outrageous charges for lodging, their trafficking and money-changing, and many other kinds of trading, they have cheated and plundered pilgrims, and so have gained wealth, they then pour contempt upon those warriors and exiles for Christ's sake, insulting them... and reproaching those who are about to fight on their own behalf...'

Thus does Jacques de Vitry, one of the outstanding Crusader theologians of his century, open the grating above the seamy nether depths of life in the Holy Land at the time. Underlying his presentation is the undoubted attempt to explain the Crusader loss of Jerusalem. He could not know that it would also do much to explain the loss of Acre and the final departure of the Crusaders some fifty years later.

The pilgrim documentation is thin for the remainder of the Crusader period. The best record, dated 1280, is that of the German monk known as Burchard of Mount Zion. The very fact that he was able to travel throughout the country, moving from Crusader to Saracen territory apparently without hindrance, throws interesting light on conditions in the land. These, after all, were the fateful years when the Mamelukes were in control of most of Palestine, including Jerusalem, having taken one coastal town and inland castle after another and pressed the Crusaders into what was now a tiny northern enclave. Yet, as he wrote, 'I have either walked on foot over the whole land, from Dan to Beersheba, from the Dead Sea to the Mediterranean Sea... or else I have carefully made inquiries from the places which I could not come at.' His writing contains no note of bitterness towards the Saracens and no hint of Saracen harshness towards the Christians. On the contrary, while he says that the Saracens 'are very unclean, and have as many wives as they can feed [even though] they practise unnatural sins and have *ephebiae* [male brothels] in every city', he finds them, nevertheless, 'very hospitable, courteous and kindly'.

In addition to describing Christian sacred sites, he gives an account of Crusader castles, and the ruins of some of the structures he mentions may be seen today. For example, he says that 'Acre is fortified with walls, outworks, towers, ditches, and barbicans of very great strength... There are in the city many strong places,

Figure of kneeling pilgrim decorating a pillar in the Church of the Nativity, Bethlehem
Right: Figure of a saint depicted on another pillar in the same church

castles and citadels belonging to the Knights of the Hospital, the Temple, and the Teutonic Order.' Acre today abounds with such Crusader remains, several of which, well preserved, have recently been excavated and restored, and are now visible and accessible.

Just south of Haifa, on the promontory of Athlit at the edge of the sea, 'is Pilgrims Castle, belonging to the Knights Templars, the most strongly fortified of all the places ever held by the Christians. It stands in the deep sea, and is fenced with walls and outworks, and such strong barbicans and towers that the whole world ought not to be able to take it.' The wall of one of its huge towers still stands to a height of 110 feet, and among the other remains are part of the southern wall, a large hall with vaulted ceiling, storage chambers, and part of a round chapel near one of the original landing stages of the harbour. It was called Pilgrims Castle as a tribute to the energetic pilgrims who helped the Templars to build it in 1218, and also because, with enough room on the promontory to serve as a transit area, it vied with Acre as a port of entry for Christian pilgrims. The Templars were happy to take away business from the Italian merchants of Acre whom they despised.

How small was the patch of territory under Crusader control in Burchard's day may be gauged by the next fortified position down the coast which he visited. This was Caesarea, which 'has a strong position, but at this day it is altogether ruined'. This coastal city was now in Saracen hands, having been captured and destroyed by the sultan Baybars in 1265. However, though Burchard saw it 'altogether ruined', the 'altogether' is not quite accurate; for a considerable excavation and restoration programme was recently undertaken, and visible today, in all its magnificence and perfection, is the undamaged Crusader moat and walled embankment which Louis IX built. Most of the surface buildings were indeed ruined by Baybars, but enough of some of the walls, gates and arches remained, and missing stones found in the debris, to make possible a remarkable restoration of the Crusader city.

Among the other castles visited by Burchard whose remains may be seen today are Montfort, some fifteen miles northeast of Acre, which 'now is utterly ruined' – to this day the most spectacular ruin in western Galilee, rising from the summit of a dominating hill above a winding brook; Castle Judin, about six miles to the south, which also 'now is ruined', having been destroyed by Baybars preparatory to his assault on Montfort; and Castle Belvoir, overlooking the Jordan south of the Sea of Galilee, which has recently been restored and is one of the most impressive Crusader sites in the country.

One final sentence from Burchard is worth quoting, as it gives some indication of the mood of the people. In his account of Jerusalem, after writing of the shrines, he says: 'At this day there are very few inhabitants for so great a city, because the people thereof dwell in continual terror.'

The Crusader castle of Montfort

9 MAMELUKE MEMORIES

In their administration of Palestine, as of their other distant provinces, the Mamelukes chose strong provincial governors, drawn from the military ranks. But to prevent their establishing themselves and consolidating their power, they were changed fairly frequently. For such local rulers, enjoying a large measure of independence and recognizing that their tenure of office would be brief, the temptation to make the most of it for personal advancement was great. Some, particularly at the beginning, undertook building programmes, notably in Jerusalem, for the glory of Islam and of the Mameluke regime. They also built a considerable network of roads and bridges, largely for military reasons and on directives from Cairo.

To the central Mameluke administration, the country was a territorial step-child. Its importance was military, as a land-bridge between Egypt and Syria, and as a buffer delaying an onslaught on Egypt should Syria be overrun; but this, it was felt, did not require an interest in the welfare of its population. This mood was naturally reflected in the attitude of later local governors. Taxation remained heavy, but more and more of such revenues found their way into the pockets of local officials (though this practice was not as common nor on as wide a scale as it became during the subsequent Ottoman regime), and little was spent on local development. Whereas at first, during the fourteenth century, for example, the Mamelukes reconstructed the Citadel in Jerusalem, added pools, repaired the aqueduct which brought water from the Hebron hills, and repaired the city walls, when these crumbled no effort was made to restore them, and fifteenth century travellers report that Jerusalem was 'without walls'. Government became lax, bribery rife, and the countryside laid open to the depredations of the Bedouin. Life became irksome for non-Moslem pilgrims and settlers, and this would be noted in the pilgrim records of the period.

Moslem pilgrims, on the other hand, found more to attract them under the Mamelukes than ever before. The Mamelukes were fine and artistic builders, and though the places holy to Islam within their dominion, notably in Cairo, Damascus

Top: Crusader, Mameluke, Ottoman and Venetian coins carried by pilgrims
Bottom: Pilgrims paying toll to Saracen guards as depicted in an illuminated medieval manuscript on pilgrimage

and Aleppo, received their main attention, they did not neglect Jerusalem. They greatly beautified the Haram esh-Sharif area by adding a number of small and attractive buildings, fountains, marble pulpits, minarets and houses of prayer; the graceful arcades which give entrance to the Dome of the Rock; and several gates to the Haram. All may be seen today. They also built four handsome madrasahs (a combination of mosque and school), and kept the Dome of the Rock and the Mosque of El-Aksa under constant repair.

By and large, the Mamelukes were tolerant of other religions. Christians and Jews were allowed freedom of worship – though there were occasional periods of persecution – and pilgrimage was permitted, though they were barred from visiting the Temple Mount in Jerusalem and the tombs of the Hebrew Patriarchs at the Cave of Machpelah in Hebron. It is also true that visits even to pilgrim sites open to both were accompanied by inconveniences and extortion. Both communities were subject to a special poll-tax, and both had to wear distinctive dress – yellow turbans for Jews, blue ones for Christians. Life for them was far from ideal, but Jews fared better than they had under the Crusaders, and Christians were better off than the Moslems had been under them.

The overall Jewish experience during the Mameluke period is one of frequent pilgrimage and of continued settlement, though the size and welfare of the community fluctuated from generation to generation. A pilgrim record at the beginning of the fourteenth century shows them contented; one at the end of the fifteenth century, during the declining years of Mameluke rule, shows them impoverished.

The 1334 record by the pilgrim Isaac ben Joseph ibn Chelo states that 'the Jewish community in Jerusalem is quite numerous... Among the different members of the holy congregation at Jerusalem are many who are engaged in handicrafts such as dyers, tailors, shoemakers, etc. Others carry on a rich commerce in all sorts of things, and have fine shops. Some are devoted to science, as medicine, astronomy and mathematics. But the greater number of their learned men are working day and night at the study of the Holy Law [the Torah and Talmud] and of the true wisdom, which is the Cabbalah [mystic interpretation of the biblical texts]. These are maintained out of the coffers of the community, because the study of the law is their only calling.' Contributing to the support of these scholars were also the Jews of the Middle East and Europe.

Ibn Chelo adds: 'There are also at Jerusalem excellent calligraphists, and the copies are sought for by the strangers, who carry them away to their own countries. I have seen a Pentateuch written with so much art that several persons at once wanted to acquire it, and it was only for an excessively high price that the Chief of the Synagogue of Babylon carried it off with him to Baghdad.'

His one doleful experience in Jerusalem is with the Temple Mount, on which he is not allowed to set foot, and when he sees the Dome of the Rock and the Mosque of El-Aksa, he cries: 'Alas, by reasons of our sins, where the sacred building

One of the tombs of the Patriarchs in the Cave of Machpelah

once stood, its place is taken today by a profane temple, built by the King of the
Ishmaelites [Moslems] when he conquered Palestine and Jerusalem from the uncircumcised [Gentiles].' But he calls 'one of the seven wonders of the Holy City
the Western Wall which stands before the Temple... The Jews resort thither to
say their prayers.'

Hebron is among the other places in Judea visited by ibn Chelo, and he wrote:
'The Jews, who are very numerous here, do a considerable trade in cotton, which
they spin and dye themselves, as well as in all sorts of glass-ware made by them
in Hebron.' (Hebron glass is still a notable product of the city, but it is now in
the hands of Arabs. Today's Jewish glass-blowers are mostly in Jerusalem.) 'They
have an ancient synagogue and pray there day and night, for they are very devout.'
Since they were forbidden access to the Cave of the Patriarchs, 'during the ten
days of penitence [between the Jewish New Year and the Day of Atonement] they
visit the tombs of Jesse, father of king David, and of Abner, son of Ner. There,
with faces turned towards the Cave of Machpelah they implore that God will
have mercy and restore this sacred place where the patriarchs are buried into their
hands, as in former days they used to be.' (This entreaty would be fulfilled only
633 years later, when, with Israel's victory in the Six Day War of June 1967, Jews
were once again able to visit their sacred shrine in Hebron.)

Eighty-seven years later, Jerusalem still had a thriving Jewish community, most
of them living in the southeast quarter of the city. Describing Jerusalem as he saw
it in 1421, the Christian pilgrim John Poloner mentioned 'the Gate of the Street
of the Jews, which gate looks out of the city to the southward... Seventy-six paces
from the aforesaid gate the street of the synagogue of the Jews extends for two
hundred and thirty-seven paces, up to the entrance to the covered streets' (i.e. to
the vaulted bazaars referred to in *La Citez de Jherusalem*). 'From this entrance it
is ninety-three paces to the Castle of David' (i.e. the Citadel), showing that it
covered much the same area as today's 'Jewish Quarter'.

The 1483 account of another Christian pilgrim, Felix Fabri, recorded that 'there
are scattered throughout the city many chapels of heretics [i.e. Christian sects other
than the Latin], many Saracen mosques, Jewish synagogues, and Samaritan tabernacles... There are more than five hundred Jews, and more than a thousand Christians, of every sect and country; but the fewest of all are they of the Latin rite.'

This figure for the Jewish community is roughly equivalent to the 'about two
hundred and fifty Jewish householders' noted in the 1481 record of the Jewish
pilgrim from Italy, Meshullam ben Menahem, who came to a Jerusalem which
'has no walls' and was very much 'in ruins'. Harsh measures by the administration
followed, and these, together with a famine which hit the land soon after, led to
the impoverishment of the community seen by Rabbi Obadiah da Bertinoro seven
years later.

This renowned Jewish scholar, noted for his Commentary on the Mishnah, made

The Jewish scribe in this photograph is writing a Torah scroll. He wears
the special garb of his calling

the pilgrimage from Italy in 1488, at a time when the general condition of the inhabitants of the land was poor and the fortunes of the Mamelukes low (their rule would end less than three decades later). His is the best Jewish record of the period.

Not only was there no development by the local administration, but there was no attempt to keep even existing buildings in repair: 'Jerusalem is for the most part desolate and in ruins... It is not surrounded by walls.' The total population of the city had dwindled to 'about 4,000 families. As for Jews', there are now only 'about seventy families of the poorest class... There is scarcely a family that is not in want of the commonest necessaries... When I came to Jerusalem there was a dreadful famine in the land...'

Rabbi Obadiah had arrived in Jerusalem on the eve of the Pilgrim Festival of Passover, and stayed to revive the Jewish community. The task was not easy. An extortionate administration made the repair of property prohibitive, and there was even Moslem encroachment upon synagogue compounds: 'In the court of the Synagogue, quite close to it, stands a mosque... At one time the Jews had more houses, but these are now heaps of rubbish and cannot be rebuilt, for the law of the land is that a Jew may not rebuild his ruined house without permission, and the permission often costs more than the whole house is worth. The houses in Jerusalem are of stone, none of wood or plaster.'

Da Bertinoro also mentioned the special taxes: 'The Jews in Jerusalem have to pay down every year thirty-two silver pieces per head. The poor man, as well as the rich, has to pay this tribute as soon as he comes to the age of manhood. Everyone is obliged to pay fifty ducats annually to the Niepo, i.e. the Governor of Jerusalem, for permission to make wine, a beverage which is an abomination to the Arabs.' (Ritual wine is required for Jewish services.)

He could not visit the Temple Mount as 'no Jew may enter the enclosure of the Temple', but he went to, and was greatly impressed by, 'the Western Wall, part of which is still standing. It is composed of large, thick stones, such as I have never before seen in an old building, either in Rome or in any other country.'

He mentions the ancient Jewish cemetery 'at the foot of the slope of the temple mountain' and 'at the foot of the Mount of Olives, and the valley [of Kidron] runs between the grave-yards. Not far from here', along the valley, 'are the monuments of Absalom and of the Prophet Zachariah' – to be seen today as they were in his day. 'On the Mount of Olives are the graves of the Prophet Haggai and Huldah the Prophetess' – their traditional burial sites are still so-marked – and 'the sepulchre of the seventy Elders' – the Sanhedrin – 'which lies about 2,000 cubits from Jerusalem, is splendid...' It still is, though it is now well inside Jerusalem, part of today's northern suburb Sanhedria, which takes its name from the sages who lie buried there.

Christian fortunes also varied throughout the period of Mameluke rule, depen-

Hand-coloured illustrated map of Jewish sacred sites
Overleaf: The Dome of the Chain on Haram esh-Sharif, adjoining the Dome of the Rock

Left: 13th century Mameluke bridge
near Lod, built by sultan Baybars·

Right: 15th century Mameluke
fountain on Haram esh-Sharif, built
by sultan Qait Bey

Above: A view of the interior of the Church of the Holy Sepulchre

Right: The first page of a Pilgrims' Register started by Franciscans in Jerusalem in the 16th century

1561

Liber Peregrinorum

Congiere ad hodiem Redi Dñs Fris Aurely Briani de ... Ordinis Minorum de Obseruat Prouincie Brixig Sacri Montis Sion Guard infrascripti ad ... Ciuitatem Hierusalem Peregrini aduenerunt

Et primo Mense Augusti eiusdem Anni 1561

Die V. Aug.	Nobilis dñs Antonius de Vegenibus Vicentinus Vtriusq; J.D.
One 03. aug d	Dñus Albertus Comes in Lewenstein, et Baro in Schauffenneck.
Eade die	Dñus Primidaus de Vickosa
Eadem die	Dñus Adrianus du Bosch.
Eadem die	Dñus Joannis Wlandensis.
Eadem die	Dñus Franciscus Reducheller
Eade die	Dñus Wlcheuart ent hez Zoe, Menrheda Frisius.
Eade die	Dñus Reimpertus de Fleinx vel Fleinx Frefen Frisius
Eade die	Eñus Bernardus à Strungin in Purge Ksin
Eade die	Dñus Joannis Christophorus Voyt a Rineck ex Vegningen
Eade die	Dñus Bartholomeus Reucuillier
Eadem die	Dñus Adamus de Teringen
Eade die	Dñus Henricus Hermanus schultzfer genad Milchling
Eadem die	Dñus Jacobus Wormser natu maior
Eadem die	Dñus Simon Viuianus Venetus Nobilis
Eadem die	Dñus Sigismundus Rumph
Eadem die	Petrus Selez Marie deViriuescha Burgensis Dicaesis Hispanus.
Eadem die	Joannis Cutia de sanct Jacobo de Palipa
Eade die	Joannis Thomas Grison de Trelic.
Eade die	Dñnus Giagnus Blanchbascon Dicaesis Rothomagensis Gallus.
Eade die	Giannis Vinaldi de Thilla ex ducatu Geldrie.
Eade die	Giannis Godschai Germanus hadelf Holandie.
Eade die	Petrus Adriani Tremper Amstodamensis.
Eade die	Theodoricus Johannis et Henricus Johannis de Purmereyed dicti ...
Eade die	Henricus Johannis et Theodoricus Johannis de Purmereydina

Aq:MALVAR

THERIAC: FINA

ding partly on the vagaries of local administrators and largely on the state of the relations between the rulers (and merchants) of the Christian West and the authorities in Cairo. Such relations were still marked by hostility in the decades immediately following the fall of Crusader Acre, for there was continued talk in Europe of a fresh Crusade, and this had its inevitable impact on the Christians in Palestine. Though, as we have seen, they were allowed freedom of worship, they were subject to the same disabilities as the Jews. They too, like the Jews, required a permit to repair a house of worship or even a dwelling, and so ecclesiastical building greatly declined; for the magnitude of the bribe to acquire a permit to construct a new church or rebuild an old one was often beyond the purse of many Christian sects, particularly those belonging to the Eastern Church. In addition, several existing churches in good repair were simply taken over by the Moslems and converted into mosques, the most notable being the Crusader Church of St Anne in Jerusalem. (It was restored to the Christians in the nineteenth century.)

In time, however, owing to the vast profitability of trade with the Levant, the influence of the western merchants proved stronger than that of the Pope, and Christian kings began making treaties with the Mameluke rulers who controlled the ports for the merchandise of the East. With such lively trade relations, Christian pilgrimage also flourished – and was seen as an additional source of revenue by the Mamelukes, though this did not markedly improve the behaviour of local officials towards the pilgrims. Insecurity and bribery were still the order of the day.

Despite these common hardships, inter-Church rivalry, particularly over the custodianship of the holy places, became even more acute. All denominations found it hard to meet extortionate payments for the right of possession and upkeep of their portions, and those with short purses eventually forfeited their rights. (The Mamelukes were quick to seize on these internal quarrels, quick to put a price upon 'concessions' in a sacred shrine, and not above playing off one sect against another.)

The Mameluke period witnessed the gradual rise of the Franciscan Order, who came to be accepted as the official representatives of the Latin Church and as guardians of the holy places on behalf of the West. Theirs is a record of much suffering and public spirit on behalf of their people, and it was they who cared for the Latin pilgrims to the Holy Land. The brothers themselves maintained their rule of poverty, but their Order became very rich, receiving both political and financial backing from the West. They were thus able to acquire land – and also extend their rights in the holy places – by out-buying or out-bidding a poorer incumbent.

Christian pilgrimage during the Mameluke period is well documented. One of the first records written only a generation after the expulsion of the Crusaders is that of Marino Sanuto, a Venetian of noble family, who was more than a simple pilgrim. At a time when the Crusading spirit was fast dying out in Europe, Sanuto

Decorated majolica jars from the famous Franciscan pharmacy in Jerusalem
which served sick pilgrims

represented the last lingering hopes of the Christian reconquest of Palestine, and the work he wrote, together with four maps, which he presented to Pope John XXI in the year 1321, was entitled *Secrets for True Crusaders to Help them Recover the Holy Land*. Though there are a good many inaccuracies both in the maps and the text, his work makes interesting reading as a combination of pilgrim guide, scriptural history and intelligence report, with occasional reference to knightly diversions, as the following brief extract illustrates: 'The order in which pilgrims visit these places is to go from Ptolemais... to Cana of Galilee, and thence to... Nazareth. Two leagues from Nazareth is Mount Tabor, where the Lord was transfigured. Here are shown the ruins of the three tabernacles which were built... There are also ruins of many other buildings, which are now the dens of lions and other wild beasts; so that here also is hunting fit for a king. The mount is hard to climb, and is very lofty, and suitable for fortification.'

Two items are worth quoting in Sanuto's account, for they provide a preliminary clue to what would very much later become one of the best known Christian traditions in Jerusalem – the Stations of the Cross. Sanuto was one of the first to mention 'the place where the Blessed Virgin fainted with grief when she beheld her innocent Son bearing His cross and distressed by its weight' – today's Fourth Station. And he also says that 'proceeding further along the aforesaid street' one reaches the spot where there was 'found one Simon of Cyrene coming from the country' who was 'compelled... to bear the cross' – today's Fifth Station.

The references to such incidents and sites are picked up by the German pastor Ludolph von Suchem in his pilgrim record of 1350; but he wrote a good deal more than Sanuto on the behaviour of the local Moslems towards Christian shrines and pilgrims. In Bethlehem, near the Church of the Nativity 'stands the monastery in which St Jerome, St Paula and Eustochium, and very many other saints once dwelt... A Saracen now dwells on this spot, and receives one Venetian penny from anyone who wants to go into the church.' He also tells of the shrines which have been converted into mosques. Passing the Church of St Anne in Jerusalem, he notes that 'the Saracens have now made [it] a church of their own'. At Gethsemane, 'a fair church stands at the place where Christ was taken, but nowadays the Saracens shut up their flocks and beasts to feed therein.' As for the Moslem attitude towards the most sacred Christian site, von Suchem says 'the Saracens have as much respect for Christ's sepulchre as Christians have for a Jewish synagogue'!

Nevertheless, he is amazed that they have not harmed the tombs in this church of the Crusader leaders Godfrey de Bouillon and his brother king Baldwin. 'It is a great wonder,' he writes, 'that the Saracens suffer their sepulchres and bodies to rest undisturbed in such honour, seeing how much harm they did them... for in Lombardy, when Christians quarrel, they cast one another's rotten corpses to the dogs.'

A wooden door on which pilgrims scratched their names in an old pilgrim hospice within St Saviour's Convent, Jerusalem

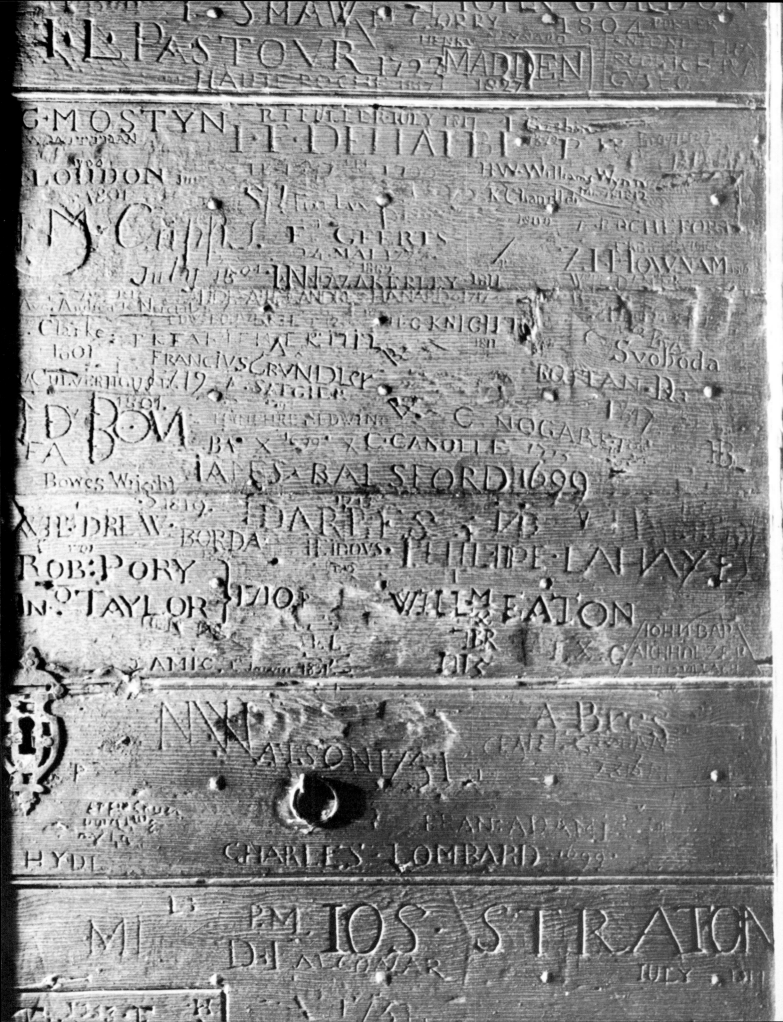

It is from von Suchem's record that we learn of the practice of locking the pilgrims in the Church of the Holy Sepulchre for 24 hours at a time, and he describes the atmosphere during a pilgrim visit: 'The church is like a palace prepared for the various needs of pilgrims and of those who are locked up therein; for pilgrims who visit it are locked up therein from the first hour of one day till the same hour of the following day, and can inspect everything to their hearts' content. Twice a year – that is to say, from Good Friday to Monday after Easter, and from the Eve of the Invention of the Holy Cross till the morrow of the feast – the Christians who dwell there are let into the church for nothing, and locked in, and then one finds shops in the church where sundry things and victuals are sold, even as in this country they do in markets and fairs, and then one hears talk and songs in divers tongues. Each several nation [sect] has its own special place for holding Divine service according to its own rite...'

The record at about the same time (1346-1350) of the noted pilgrim, Fra Niccolo of Poggibonsi, who belonged to the Franciscans, or Friars Minor, also reported on the Saracenic practice of regulating visits to Jerusalem's central church by locking in the pilgrims. And one hundred and fifty years later, they were subjected to the same procedure, as we learn from the 1494 account of the Italian priest and scholar, Canon Pietro Casola. He wrote: 'You must know that although the Sepulchre is governed by the Friars of Mount Zion and by other sects of Christians, nevertheless they cannot go in or out at pleasure, but must do so at the pleasure of that dog who always keeps the keys. He is the Moor who auctions the tolls on the pilgrims and on those who wish to visit the Sepulchre even at other times.' In this way, the Moslems both underlined their authority and ensured that none evaded payment of fees all along the line – from the moment they stepped foot in the country.

Casola recited a long tale of woe concluding with this piece of advice to pilgrims: 'Each one who goes on the voyage to the Sepulchre of our Lord has need of three sacks – a sack of patience, a sack of money and a sack of faith.'

This is the characteristic note of all the pilgrim records which have come down to us from the fourteenth and fifteenth centuries, the most important of which, apart from the ones already mentioned, being those of the credulous Sir John Maundeville (about 1356); the three very lively Florentines, Frescobaldi, Gucci and Sigoli (1384); the urbane Burgundian Bertrandon de la Brocquiere (1432); and the meticulous German Dominican Felix Fabri (1483).

All, as part of their pilgrimage experience during this Mameluke period, suffered the irksomeness of Moslem bureaucracy, high-handedness, insecurity, and the innumerable tolls, fees, charges and outright bribes in their efforts to see the Christian holy places. Even when things went well, as they did with the wealthy de la Brocquiere, there were frustrating delays, red tape and endless payments. After

Carved panels marked by pilgrim names on a door in St Catherine's
Monastery, Sinai

accomplishing all the usual visits in Jerusalem, he and a group of ten pilgrims, distinguished noblemen in the states of the Duke of Burgundy, 'undertook another pilgrimage, equally customary, to St Catherine's Monastery' in the Sinai desert. 'For the information of others, who, like myself, may wish to visit this country, I shall say that the custom is to treat with the chief interpreter [head of the guides] at Jerusalem, who receives a tax for the sultan, and one for himself, and then sends to inform the interpreter at Gaza, who, in his turn, negotiates a passage with the Arabians of the desert. These Arabs enjoy the right of conducting pilgrims; and... their camels must be used, which they let to hire at ten ducats a head. The Saracen who at this time held the office of chief interpreter... having received the answer from the Arabs, he called us together... and he took down in writing our ages, names, surnames, and very particular descriptions of our persons, and sent a duplicate of this to the chief interpreter at Cairo. These precautions are taken for the security of travellers, and to prevent the Arabs from detaining any of them; but I am persuaded that it is done likewise through mistrust, and through fear of some exchange or substitution that may make them lose the tribute-money.'

The earlier and impecunious Fra Niccolo told what happened when the Moslem officials feared they might 'lose the tribute-money', recounting a grim tale of arrest and beatings when his interpreter explained that 'we had no money, and that as friars of Mount Zion we carried neither gold nor silver'. He was saved only through the intervention of an influential Christian, and his Order later paid 'the Sultan's tribute'.

Incidentally, the record of Fra Niccolo is of particular interest to ecclesiastical historians for his cataloguing of the indulgences associated with each of the Christian shrines. For example, inside the Church of the Holy Sepulchre, he described the stone where Jesus was anointed and embalmed, and added: 'And at the above-mentioned stone there is a plenary indulgence.' The chapel of the Sepulchre also carries 'a plenary indulgence'. At the place where Jesus appeared to Mary Magdalene, 'there is an indulgence of 7 years'; and at the place where he was imprisoned, 'there is an indulgence of 7 years and 70 days'.

Whatever the experience of the pilgrims once they reached Palestine, getting there was often far more dramatic. This was always so, since the early centuries, for sea travel was hazardous, and so was the desert trek through Sinai for those who had landed on the coast of Egypt. But unlike the earlier records, which with certain exceptions tend to plunge directly into a description of the holy places, several pilgrim reports of the fourteenth and fifteenth centuries offered detailed accounts of the journey from Europe, and one gets the full flavour of what it was like to be a pilgrim in those days.

Visitors to St Catherine's Monastery were hoisted through a special 'security entrance' in times of danger

10 THE HAZARDS OF PILGRIMAGE

Travel, as we would expect, was less arduous towards the end of the Mameluke period. Da Bertinoro, for example, making the pilgrimage in 1488, offered only a passing mention of the journey: 'Every year Jews come in the Venetian galleys... for there is really no safer and shorter way than in these ships...'

A century earlier, journeying to the Holy Land was far less safe, and 'such a passage as from here [Venice] to Alexandria would harm the robust body of any sailor'. This we learn from the most vivid account of the period, the pilgrim record of three noblemen of Florence, Leonardo Frescobaldi, Giorgio Gucci and Simone Sigoli, who, together with ten other Tuscans (three of whom died later en route), set forth from Venice at the beginning of September 1384. They embarked on a vessel laden with 'Lombard cloth, silver bullion, copper, oil and saffron,' and carrying 'merchants and pilgrims and soldiers' – the soldiers being 'fifteen good bowmen' whom 'the captain had engaged, besides those for the service of the ship'. This was a wealthy group who could afford to travel in a vessel that 'was new and large' and which had been built 'to make fun of the sea'. And, indeed, their voyage was less of a trial than it was for pilgrims of more slender means. They came across one such group of unfortunates just after setting sail. Moving through the gulf of Venice, they encountered a 'small tempest' which they weathered quite easily; 'but an unarmed galley, laden with pilgrims returning from the Sepulchre, since it was old, opened, and about two hundred, all poor people, perished; and to pay little, they had boarded such a bad vessel, as it so often happens that worse arrangements are for the poor.'

Despite this depressing incident, they went ahead, successfully negotiating places where 'very many ships, both small and great, were lost', and experiencing their worst moments only when they neared Alexandria. There, 'we were in such distress that in hell you could not have more, for the cock-boat was all the time tossed on its sides by the winds, so that now one side went in the air, and the other to earth, one by turn going up and the other down, without having ever a moment of rest or repose.'

Pilgrims arriving at Alexandria would go by barque from Rosetta down the

Nile to Cairo and start their overland journey to Palestine from there. 'We furnished ourselves to cross the desert with two bushels of biscuits, according to our measure, and we were between us and domestics, the interpreter and cameleers, eighteen mouths. The grand interpreter' – the most senior official in Cairo in charge of all the pilgrim arrangements – 'took from us for the passage 96 gold ducats, and wished many other things from us. He lent or had lent to us 14 camels, which are almost wild, and the grand interpreter took from us for carriage 96 ducats... We bought 3 riding donkeys for us... a small tent under which to spend the night, and we provided ourselves with vinegar and with plenty of sugar and cheese.'

They also bought 'goat-skins and leather flasks, and other utensils... and on 19th October [1384] before dawn' they left Cairo. Journeying through country which 'was a bank of stones burned by the sun', the Florentines 'met a caravan of French gentlemen pilgrims, among whom were five knights with gold spurs, who, frightened, asked us how many of us were dead so far. We replied that only one, whom God had called to himself... They told us that twenty knights had set out in company and that eleven were dead; and that some we have buried in the sand.'

A few days later they reached 'the foot of the Holy Mounts' – the 'Mountain of Moses' and 'Mount Sinai' – and spent a few days at the Monastery of St Catherine. They then pressed on towards Gaza, a journey which took another twelve days.

Gucci gives a more detailed description of their daily routine and of the atmosphere of desert travel. 'Either on beast or on foot it is tiresome because a man sticks beyond measure in this sand. All this land is without inhabitants or houses, and it is sterile in water. You find only pilgrims and... caravans, that is, herds of camels on the way from the Red Sea... loaded with spices... because from India many times a year many big ships, laden with spices, come by this Red Sea... And this is how we crossed the said desert; some of us were riding on camels, and some on asses, which had saddles and stirrups of rope. And... we arose and rolled up the mattresses on which we slept... and we arranged all our things and equipment, and we loaded it on the camels and asses. And we took about one hour and a half from rising before being able to continue our way; and yet, we travelled several miles before day-break. And we travelled all day, and never rested until the 22nd hour... and we encamped wherever camping time found us. And we unloaded the animals and our things; and pitched a leather pavilion... and we slept on small light mattresses, and sometimes they sank into the sand so that we slept as much on the sand as on the mattresses. Nevertheless at night as we slept, one of us would mount guard... We had of water a little, because in such journeys you must make an economy; and then it was bad, for, although we put good water in the skins, it at once took the taste of the skin and the fat of the leather, and it came out full of the hairs of the beast, found inside the skins. And such was our life through the desert; and our refreshed days, from one to the other, were from 22 to 26 miles a day.'

The ancient Chapel of the Burning Bush — and part of the 'Bush' itself — in St Catherine's Monastery
Overleaf: 15th century representation of Master Conterini's Venetian pilgrim galley

Three weeks after leaving Cairo, they were robbed. 'In the said desert, on the 11th day of November, we came across several Saracens on horse and on foot with dogs, as if they were going on the hunt, and, pretending to be officials of the grand interpreter of the Arabs, they said they wished to check our receipts and safe-conducts and right away began to push our camels out of the straight route, and to take clothes, mantles, hats, wax and many other things, pilfering by force, and in the end compelled us to ransom ourselves for about 15 ducats and gave us back the greater part of the things wrested from us.'

On reaching Gaza they rested up for several days and then journeyed to Jerusalem travelling via Hebron where they met 'many Jews from many lands who came in pilgrimage to the said city'. Thence to Bethlehem and their final destination.

A hundred years later, Brother Felix Fabri joined some 'nobles of the country who wished to make the pilgrimage', serving them as chaplain, and reached Venice from Ulm in Germany in April 1483. His account shows that towards the end of the Mameluke period, pilgrimage was well organized, both in Europe and in Palestine. Venice was the centre of the pilgrimage movement and the pilgrims went on what today would be called 'package tours', the price covering the round trip fare, a stay in the Holy Land and the fees for the places visited on the 'Holy Circuit'.

In Venice, masters of galleys vied with each other for business, each claiming that his vessel was both more comfortable and less expensive. They drew up careful contracts with travelling groups which had to be approved by the Venetian authorities, and which included such items as the tariff to be paid to a local guide and the waiting time at port of destination before returning.

The party of Brother Felix were approached for their custom by Master Augustine Conterini and Master Peter de Lando, two ship-owners to whom the Lords of Venice 'entrusted the care of the pilgrims'. On inspection, Conterini's vessel was found to be 'only double-banked, and less roomy, and withal old and stinking', and so they decided to travel with Master Peter whose vessel was 'a three-banked galley, large and broad, and besides this, new and clean'. A twenty-article contract was thereupon drawn up between the Master and the pilgrims and endorsed by the Venetian authorities. Here are some of its provisions:

'First Article: That the captain shall take us pilgrims from Venice to Joppa, a port in the Holy Land, and shall bring us back again from thence to Venice...

Second: That he shall well and properly provide a galley with experienced mariners who understand the art of sailing with whatever wind may blow, and shall have on board a sufficient armament for the defence of the galley from the attacks of pirates and enemies, if need be...

Fifth: That the captain shall be bound to provide the pilgrims, during their voyage from Venice to the Holy Land, and from thence back to Venice, with a sufficiency of good bread and biscuit, good wine and sweet water, freshly put on board, with meat, eggs, and other eatables of the same sort.

A nineteenth-century pilgrim (followed by porter and guide) arriving at Casa Nova, the new pilgrim hospice opened by Franciscans in 1850

Sixth: That every morning before we eat our food he shall give to each of us a bicker or small glass of Malvoisie wine, as is the custom on shipboard...

Ninth: The captain shall be bound to protect the pilgrims, both in the galley and out of it, from being attacked or ill-used by the galley-slaves... He shall also be bound to prevent the slaves from molesting them on land, as far as he is able, and he shall not place any article in the pilgrims' berths.

Tenth: The captain shall let the pilgrims remain in the Holy Land for the due length of time, and shall not hurry them through it too fast, and shall lead them to the usual places and go with them in person. We especially wish him to raise no objections to leading them to the Jordan, which pilgrims always find a difficulty in doing, and he shall save them from all troubles with the infidels.

Eleventh: All dues, all money for safe-conducts, and for asses and other expenses, in whatever names they may be charged, or in whatever place they have to be paid, shall be paid in full by the captain alone on behalf of all the pilgrims without their being charged anything, and he shall likewise pay the great fees; the smaller fees we will see to ourselves.

Twelfth: In return for all these expenses to be incurred and things to be done by the captain, each pilgrim shall be bound to pay forty ducats of the kind called *de Zecha*, that is, newly minted. On condition, however, that the pilgrim shall pay one-half of this sum in Venice, and the remainder at Joppa...

Eighteenth: That the captain shall assign to the pilgrims some convenient place on board of the galley for keeping chickens or fowls, and that his cooks shall permit the pilgrims' cook to use their fire for cooking for the pilgrims at their pleasure.

Nineteenth: Should any pilgrim on board of the galley happen to fall so ill as not to be able to remain in the stench of the cabin, the captain shall be bound to give such a person some place to rest in on the upper deck, either in the castle, the poop, or one of the rowers' benches...'

They arrived at Jaffa on 2 July 1483 and waited on board for three days until 'safe-conduct' papers were brought from Jerusalem by the 'Father Guardian of Mount Zion' and they were allowed to go ashore. Brother Felix describes the landing:

'Above us stood the Father Guardian of Mount Zion and his brethren together, with the governors of the land, and the elders of the Saracens and Moors, and with a scribe; and they had so ranged themselves on either side that the pilgrims must needs pass through the midst of them... one after the other. Nor would they let us pass in a continuous stream, but they laid hold of each man, looked at him narrowly, and demanded his own name and the name of his father both of which names the scribe wrote down in his documents.'

After registration the pilgrims were put into caverns, under heavy Saracen guard, for four days and nights. They were then ordered to prepare themselves for the journey to Jerusalem. After they had hired asses, the caravan set off, encamping

Russian pilgrims at a mass baptismal ceremony on the banks of the Jordan at the turn of the century

the first night at Ramla. Here they were given a list of 'do's and don'ts' at a briefing by the Father Guardian of Mount Zion. His exhortations show how frightened and insecure were the minorities in the land, and how careful they had to be not to cross the local Moslems. The pilgrims were accepted on sufferance and treated with contempt by the Moslems even while they were extorting fees and bribes from the visitors. The twenty-seven 'articles wherein were contained the rules and method... which they ought to observe while dwelling among Saracens and infidels in the Holy Land' are very revealing of the state of affairs in the country at the time. Here are some of the more illuminating of these fifteenth century directives on pilgrim behaviour which Felix Fabri records:

'...Second article: No pilgrim ought to wander alone about the holy places without a Saracen guide, because this is dangerous and unsafe...

Third: The pilgrim should beware of stepping over the sepulchres of the Saracens, because they are greatly vexed when they see this done, and pelt with stones anyone who steps over them...

Fourth: Should any pilgrim be struck by a Saracen, however unjustly, he must not return the blow...

Fifth: Let the pilgrims beware of chipping off fragments from the holy Sepulchre, and from the buildings at other places, and spoiling the hewn stones thereof...

Sixth: Pilgrims of noble birth must not deface walls by drawing their coats-of-arms thereon, or by writing their names, or by fixing upon the walls papers on which their arms are painted, or by scratching columns and marble slabs, or boring holes in them with iron tools, to make marks of their having visited them; for such conduct gives great offence to the Saracens, and they think those who do so to be fools...

Eighth: Pilgrims must beware of laughing together as they walk about Jerusalem to see the holy places, but they must be grave and devout, both on account of the holy places, and of the example which they afford to the infidels, and also lest the latter should suspect that we are laughing at them, which annoys them exceedingly. They are always suspicious about laughter and merriment among pilgrims.

Ninth: Let the pilgrims beware above all of jesting with or laughing at the Saracen boys or men whom they may meet, because, however well meant this conduct may be, yet much mischief arises from it...

Tenth: Let the pilgrim beware of gazing upon any women whom they may meet, because all Saracens are exceeding jealous, and a pilgrim may in ignorance run himself into danger through the fury of some jealous husband.

Eleventh: Should any woman beckon to a pilgrim or invite him by signs to enter a house, let him on no account do so, because the woman does this treacherously at the instigation of some men, in order that the Christian when he enters may be robbed, and perhaps slain. Those who are not careful in these matters incur great danger.

A religious souvenir shop adjoining the Church of the Holy Sepulchre

Twelfth: Let every pilgrim beware of giving a Saracen wine when he asks for drink, whether on the roadside or elsewhere, because straightway after one single draught thereof he becomes mad, and the first man whom he attacks is the pilgrim who gave it him...

Sixteenth: No pilgrim may wear knives or anything else slung about him, lest they be torn from him and carried off, nor may he bear any arms whatsoever.

Seventeenth: Should any pilgrim form a friendship with any Saracen, he must beware of trusting him too far, for they are treacherous...

Eighteenth: Let every pilgrim carefully guard his own property, and never leave it lying about in any place where Saracens are, otherwise it will straightway vanish, whatever it may be...

Twentieth: Let no Christian have money dealings with a Saracen except in such sort that he knows he cannot be cheated; for they strive to cheat us...

Twenty-first: When pilgrims make convenants with Saracens, let them not dispute with them, nor swear at them, nor become angry with them...

Twenty-second: Let the pilgrim beware of entering mosques, that is, Saracen temples and oratories, because if he be found therein, he will in no case escape unharmed, even should he escape with his life...

Twenty-fourth: If a pilgrim be detained longer than he wishes in Rama [Ramla] or elsewhere, let him endure it with patience, and not think it to be the fault of the Father Guardian, but of the Saracens, who do what they please in these matters, not what is convenient to us.

Twenty-fifth: Pilgrims must not grudge to pay money to save themselves from the many annoyances which beset them, but when money has to be paid they must give it straightway without grumbling...

Twenty-seventh and last article: The pilgrims must show respect to the poor convent of the brethren of Mount Zion in Jerusalem, by whose help pilgrims are conducted into and out of the Holy Land, and must by their alms cherish this convent and help the brethren thereof, who dwell there among the infidels for the comfort of pilgrims, and who are willing to serve pilgrims according to their means, even by laying themselves down beneath their feet if necessary...'

After recording this list of the Father Guardian's directives, Fabri adds: 'These articles were read aloud to the pilgrims, both in Latin and in German. Now, as the sermon lasted so long, the Saracens, who were shut out from us in the outer court, became impatient, and beat upon the door with stones as though they would break it down. Others mounted upon the house-top and looked down upon the court where we were, laughing and shouting.' Thus, the pilgrims had an immediate foretaste of the local attitude towards them, and this Moslem behaviour towards non-Moslem pilgrims remained unchanged throughout the centuries when the Mamelukes were in power and during the Ottoman period which followed.

Jaffa Gate at the beginning of the century

1835 water-colour of English pilgrims, travelling with local guide, interpreter and baggage-master, being shown skeletons of stylites

Right: Photographs from an American family archive of a 1907 pilgrimage
Top: Bethany. Centre: A halt between Jericho and Jerusalem. Bottom: En route north

11 MODERN TIMES

Mameluke dominion over Palestine ended in the final days of the year 1516 with its conquest by the Ottoman Turks, the new imperial Moslem power which held ·sway over Asia Minor, parts of Europe and the Balkans, and which now added Syria and Egypt to its empire. The victorious sultan, Selim 1 (1512-1520), made a ceremonial entry into Jerusalem, and for the next four hundred years the Holy Land was to remain an Ottoman domain, administered by Turkish officers as governors of its five districts.

The features of this administration – lack of interest in local development, indifference to the needs of the inhabitants, extortionate taxation and widespread corruption – were to mark all but the first few decades of the Ottoman period. The most constructive impact was exerted in the opening years by the son of the sultan Selim. He was Suleiman the Magnificent (or the Lawgiver, as he was known in Turkey), who reigned from 1520 to 1566, and his most notable accomplishments in the country are still to be seen in the Jerusalem of today. It was he who restored the ramparts of the Old City, and the walls we now see are the walls, virtually unchanged, which he rebuilt. Today's Damascus Gate, one of the most elaborate of all the city gates, is Suleiman's structure. He also added decorative adornments to the Haram esh-Sharif, particularly to the Dome of the Rock, erected public fountains in the city, restored dams and aqueducts and generally improved the water services.

The Mameluke practice of dunning Christians and Jews for a special poll tax was continued, but both were left free to conduct their communal affairs and enjoyed freedom of worship. Under Suleiman's good administration, and with rising prosperity in the country, they too fared reasonably well (though towards the end of his reign both were denied residence on Mount Zion, traditional site, for Jews, of David's tomb, and, for Christians, of the Coenaculum, scene of the Last Supper).

In Suleiman's time, Jews living in lands within the Ottoman empire were relatively free of the persecution they suffered at the hands of the Christians in Spain, Portugal, Germany and central Europe. There was no Ottoman Inquisition; and when the Jewish communities in Spain were expelled in 1492 and from Portugal

Greek Orthodox ceremony of the Washing of the Feet in the entrance courtyard of the Church of the Holy Sepulchre shown in an 1871 photograph

four years later, unable to escape to France because the frontier was closed, they fled by sea to Italy, to North Africa and to the Levant. They then faced persecution in Italy. In Palestine, however, they could practise their religion, and many reached the Holy Land at this time, flocking to Safad and Tiberias in the Galilee and to Jerusalem in Judea and creating new centres of settlement and talmudic study.

Vestiges of efficient administration enjoyed under Suleiman were evident in the immediate years following his death, but decline set in towards the end of the century, and except for the five-year governorship of Mohammed Pasha from 1620 to 1625, Ottoman rule in Palestine for the next three hundred years was to be marked by neglect and corruption, which had their inevitable effect on pilgrimage.

The general atmosphere was one of decay. The land slid into ruin. Trees were cut down and villages destroyed when farmers were unable to meet the tax demands of the local pashas. Cultivable areas went to waste and fields still standing were laid open to Bedouin. In the urban centres, permits to build or repair became even more exorbitant – and so did the bribes to secure the permits. The installation of a new governor meant additional fees for renewed permits, and fresh bribes.

It was against this pattern of Ottoman corruption that the various Christian sects, instead of uniting in common adversity, sharpened their internal rivalries. Each tried to increase its powers and extend its rights at the expense of the others. The principal and most powerful contenders were the Latins and the Greek Orthodox, with the latter seeking to recover ground lost to the Latins during the Crusader period when they achieved supremacy over the holy places. The Greek Orthodox and the other sects belonging to the Eastern Church were more successful, as they had more followers than did the westerners among Ottoman subjects, and these included officials at the sultan's court. Indeed, the Latins might have been ousted if it were not for their wealth, their constant supply of profitable pilgrims, and, later, their political influence, securing the protection of European powers, notably France, with whom the Ottomans wished to remain friendly. (The Orthodox Church balanced this towards the end of the eighteenth century by gaining the protection of the Russian Czars.) There was also rivalry among the Eastern sects.

These sectarian quarrels were the subject of report and comment in all the pilgrim records of the Ottoman period. The account of *Fourteen Englishmen in Company* who made the pilgrimage in 1669 relates that members of the various sects who have rights in the Church of the Holy Sepulchre 'live there continually... The Greeks and Latins are the two powerful Religions in the temple, and with great sums of money, and credit they have at Constantinople, they continually buy these Holy Places out of another's hands; the other parties are poor, and are therefore squeezed into a small part of the temple. The Latins once offered ten thousand livres for a piece of the Cross, which the Greeks bought out of their hands. These religious people bear little respect one to another, speaking very basely each of the other.'

Greek Orthodox Easter procession along Via Dolorosa
Overleaf: American fundamentalist sect rapt in prayer at the Garden Tomb in Jerusalem

The situation worsened with time. The noted British Prelate Henry Maundrell made the pilgrimage in 1697 and he wrote of the 'unchristian fury and animosity, especially between the Greeks and Latins', over which 'the several sects [contend for] the command and appropriation of the Holy Sepulchre'. He adds that 'in disputing which party should go into it to celebrate their mass, they have sometimes proceeded to blows and wounds even at the very door of the sepulchre, mingling their own blood with their sacrifices, in evidence of which fury the father guardian showed us a great scar upon his arm, which he told us was the mark of a wound given him by a sturdy Greek priest in one of these unholy wars.' Some hundred and fifty years later, in 1845, another Englishman, Canon George Williams, could still write of 'the bitter hostility which prevails among the various denominations of Christians in the Holy City'.

In 1757, the Ottoman Government drew up *The Status Quo in the Holy Places*, which carefully prescribed the rights and possessions of the different denominations, right down to such details as who was allowed to clean the steps of the Chapel of Calvary, which parts of the rotunda of the Sepulchre were to be controlled by whom, how many lamps each could have, and where, and how high or low they could be hung. This status quo, which has undergone only slight changes since it was promulgated, still left ample scope for continued conflict, and was the subject of incessant pressures at the sultan's court by the different sects to change it in their favour.

Although, as we have seen, western pilgrims were mostly critical of the Eastern denominations, their records show least bitterness towards the Armenians. Maundrell, who viewed the country and the people with a very sober eye, was much taken with them and highly impressed with their Church of St James in Jerusalem. 'The Armenians have here a very large and delightful space of ground', with 'convent and gardens… within the walls of the city.' They still do, and the 'Armenian Quarter' is still the best kept – and the cleanest – part of the Old City. Maundrell continued: 'In this church are two altars set out with extraordinary splendour, being decked with rich mitres, embroidered copes, crosses both silver and gold, crowns, chalices, and other church utensils without number. In the middle of the church is a pulpit made of tortoise-shell and mother of pearl, with a beautiful canopy or cupola over it of the same fabric. The tortoise-shell and mother of pearl are so exquisitely mingled and inlaid in each other that the work far exceeds the materials.' Much of this may be seen in the church today, but their most precious treasures are kept in vaults. In 1969, for the first time on record, the Armenians brought forth these treasures and, with the help of the Israel Museum, put them on public display at a special exhibition in a hall near the Armenian Patriarchate. The copes and crosses, mitres and chalices enchanted the modern visitors as much as they did the seventeenth century Maundrell, but most impressive of all, particularly for scholars and art-lovers, were the magnificent illuminated manuscripts,

Precious mitre from the ancient treasures of the Armenian Patriarchate in Jerusalem accumulated over many centuries, which are part of the priceless library of the Armenian Church.

It was during this period, as we have observed earlier, that the tradition of the Via Dolorosa and the Stations of the Cross was established, and its development may be followed in the successive pilgrim reports. Indeed, the tradition is largely the product of pilgrimage, the organized tour along the 'Way of the Cross' eventually evolving into a ritual, and specific events associated with the painful progress of Jesus from judgement to crucifixion being formally marked by 'Stations'.

It was at the end of the thirteenth and beginning of the fourteenth centuries that there were faint stirrings of the tradition. In the next two centuries, several events believed to have occurred along the route to the crucifixion were mentioned by pilgrims, though their locations varied. Only in the middle of the nineteenth century were the events and their locations precisely defined, with the establishment of the Fourteen Stations as we know them today.

The first two Stations are placed in Antonia, the next seven along the route, and the last five within the Church of the Holy Sepulchre. Each is now marked by a chapel, part of a column or just a sign, and today one moves from one to the other through the narrow, winding, cobbled alleyways of the markets of the Old City.

The First Station, marking the spot where Jesus was sentenced, now lies within the courtyard of the Umariya Boys' School, some three hundred yards from the Lions' Gate. The Second, in the lane just opposite the Chapel of the Condemnation, is where Jesus is said to have received the cross. The Third, commemorating Jesus' first fall, is marked by a broken column, now part of a renovated chapel. The Fourth, where Jesus met his mother, is marked by an altar adjoining the Armenian Catholic Church of Our Lady of the Spasm. The Fifth, marked by a Franciscan oratory, is where the cross was laid upon Simon of Cyrene. The Sixth, where Veronica wiped the face of Jesus, is marked by a fragment of a column inserted into the wall of a Greek Catholic chapel. The Seventh is where Jesus fell the second time and is marked by a Franciscan chapel. The Eighth, where Jesus spoke to the compassionate daughters of Jerusalem, is denoted by a cross set in the wall of the Greek Orthodox Convent of St Charalambos. The Ninth, where Jesus fell the third time, is marked by the pillar of the door of the Coptic Church. The Tenth, already inside the Church of the Holy Sepulchre, is where Jesus was stripped of his garments, and is marked by the Latin Chapel of Calvary. The Eleventh, where Jesus was nailed to the cross, is the mosaic above the altar of that chapel. The Twelfth, where the cross was erected and where Jesus died, is located below the altar of the adjoining Greek Orthodox Chapel of Calvary. The Thirteenth commemorates the taking down of the body and is marked by the Latin 'altar of the Stabat Mater' between the Eleventh and Twelfth Stations. The fourteenth, where Jesus was laid to rest, is the Holy Sepulchre itself.

A. MOUNT MORIAH.   B. MOUNT ZION.

A.1 *Mount of Olives.*	11 *Hill of Evil Council.*	21.21 *Via Dolorosa.*
2 *Road to Bethany.*	12 *House of Caiphas.*	22 *Fish Market.*
3 *Place where Jesus wept.*	13 *Aaceldama, or field of Blood.*	23 *St. Stephen's Gate.*
4 *Garden of Gethsemane.*	14 *The Temple.*	24 *Fish Gate.*
5.5 *Valley of Jehoshaphat.*	15 *Golden Gate.*	25 *Old Gate.*
6.6 *Brook Kedron.*	16 *Porch of Solomon.*	26 *Gate of Ephrem.*
7 *Point of Ascension.*	17.17 *Pool of Bethesda.*	27 *Gate of Herod.*
8 *Absalom's Pillar.*	18 *Aqueduct.*	28 *Hebron Gate.*
9 *The Village of Siloam.*	19 *Road to Bethlehem.*	29 *Gate of Esseans.*
10 *Hill of Offence.*	20.20 *Tower of Antonia.*	30 *Zion Gate.*

DUBOURG'S OR

ANCIENT

A.D.

James M

AL VIEW OF

JERUSALEM

65.

ershaw

OR.

L

C. UPPER CITY.		D. BEZETHA.			
31	*Sheep Market.*	41	*The Lower Court.*	51	*Great Market.*
32	*Tower of Acra.*	42	*Upper Court.*	52	*Dung Gate.*
33	*Tower of Hippicus.*	43	*Hall of Judgment.*	53	*Palace of the Kings.*
34	*Calvary.*	44	*Pilate's House.*	54	*Circus.*
35	*Holy Sepulchre.*	45	*Tyropean Valley.*	55	*Theatre.*
36	*Pool of Hezekiah.*	46	*High Bridge.*	56.56.56	*Valley of Ghion.*
37	*Palace of Helena.*	47	*Solomon's Gate.*	57	*Upper Pool of Ghion.*
38	*Tower of Psephnia.*	48	*Hippodrome.*	58	*Road to Joppa.*
39	*Judgment Gate.*	49	*Xystus.*	59	*Wilderness of St. John.*
40	*Tower of Phasœlus.*	50	*Prison.*	60	*Bethlehem.*

Above: Simhat Torah (Rejoicing of the Law) celebration after the Six Day War in Jerusalem

Right: Prayers at the Western Wall on the Pilgrim Festival of Succot after the Six Day War. Worshippers carry etrog (citron) and lulav (palm branch)

The administration became more harsh and oppressive; yet pilgrimage continued, Christian as well as Jewish – and so did Jewish settlement, despite the disabilities, restrictions, extortion and humiliation. Twenty years after the death of Suleiman, the local pasha could seize the principal synagogue in Jerusalem, the thirteenth century synagogue of Nahmanides (The Ramban), and turn it into a mosque. (After painful effort and bribery, the Jews established another synagogue on the traditional site of the synagogue of the first century sage, Rabbi Yohanan ben Zakkai, which was, in our own day, the oldest synagogue in Jerusalem and in continuous use since the sixteenth century. It was destroyed by the Jordanians in 1948 and restored only after the Six Day War.)

The pilgrim reports of the next century show that confiscation was only one of the travails the Jews had to suffer. A frequent indulgence of Mohammed ibn-Farouk, who followed the benign Mohammed Pasha in 1625, was to order his troops to surround a synagogue on the Sabbath, seize the leading worshippers and hold them for high ransom. When payment was slow – the community found it difficult to raise large sums – the detainees would be brought to the synagogue and tortured before the eyes of the congregation. They were forced to sell or pledge their household chattels to speed the release of the detainees. On one occasion, after the ransom had been paid, the community was given a little time to recover and then the pasha ordered the synagogue to be impounded and converted into a profane storehouse – unless a large additional payment was forthcoming. 'Today', recorded a pilgrim at the time, the Jews in the country 'are mortgaged – men, women and children – to the Ishmaelite dwellers of this Land.'

Yet still they came, both as pilgrims and as settlers. Indeed, one of the remarkable phenomena of the Ottoman period was the survival – and growth – of the Jewish community in Palestine, their main centres being Jerusalem, Safad, Tiberias and Hebron. In 1701, Rabbi Yehuda He'Hassid arrived in the country with a thousand Jews from Poland. They established themselves in Jerusalem near the Western Wall 'and bought a house in the holy enclosure' of a synagogue, as Rabbi Gedalia, one of Rabbi Yehuda's companions, recorded at the time. 'The enclosure had several buildings within it, about forty houses and also a study hall... a ritual bath... and a house for the poor.' Rabbi Yehuda died shortly after his arrival, but his friends continued with his plans to enlarge the synagogue and study hall, 'and very large sums have been spent on the synagogue... and many bribes as well... For such are the ways of the kingdom of the Ishmaelites'. But the bribes were not enough, and in 1720, when the buildings were completed, 'the leaders of the Ishmaelites imposed on the members of the group heavy taxes which they could not pay', and looted the silver vessels, burnt the synagogue and tore down the adjoining buildings. The stone shell of the synagogue remained, and was known ever after as the 'Hurva', Hebrew for 'ruin', and only more than a century later was permission secured for its reconstruction. (It was again destroyed, in 1948, by the Jordanian Arab Legion. With its recovery by Israel in the Six Day War, plans are being prepared for its restoration.)

A report on the scale of pilgrimage and the state of the land in the middle of the eighteenth century is given by the Swedish traveller Frederick Hasselquist, who visited the country in 1751. After recording his payment of 'the twenty-two piasters which every Frank is obliged to pay... for the privilege of coming on shore and travelling in the country', he adds: 'As 4,000 persons' – the reference is to Christians – 'arrive yearly, besides as many Jews, who come from all quarters of the world, this may be esteemed a considerable revenue for the Turks; and indeed they receive no other from this uncultivated and almost uninhabited country.'

The following century saw a considerably larger annual pilgrimage than Hasselquist's 8,000 Christians and Jews, and, indeed, the nineteenth century pilgrim records are rich and numerous. The one with the lightest touch is that by the sophisticated Englishman, Alexander William Kinglake, in 1835, and he represents the new kind of pilgrim who was emerging in this period of improved and more comfortable travel from the west, one who was prompted by the religious impulse but who was also out to enjoy the voyage. Thus, relaxing after many visits to the sacred sites, he sheds his pilgrim garb and offers us this view of Jerusalem: 'If you stay in the Holy City long enough to fall into anything like regular habits of amusement and occupation, and to become for a time, in short, "a man about town", you will necessarily lose the enthusiasm which you may have felt when you trod the sacred soil for the first time, and it will then seem almost strange to you to find yourself so entirely surrounded in all your daily pursuits by the signs and sounds of religion. Your hotel is a monastery, your rooms are cells, the landlord is a stately abbot, and the waiters are hooded monks. If you walk out of the town you find yourself on the Mount of Olives, or in the Valley of Jehoshaphat, or on the Hill of Evil Counsel. If you mount your horse and extend your rambles, you will be guided to the Wilderness of St John, or the birthplace of our Saviour. Your club is the great Church of the Holy Sepulchre, where everybody meets everybody every day. If you lounge through the town, your Pall Mall is the Via Dolorosa, and the object of your hopeless affections is some maid or matron all forlorn, and sadly shrouded in her pilgrim's robes. If you would hear music, it must be the chanting of friars. If you look at pictures, you see Virgins with misforeshortened arms, or devils out of drawings, or angels tumbling up the skies in impious perspective. If you would make any purchases, you must go again to the church doors; and when you inquire for the manufactures of the place you find that they consist of double-blessed beads and sanctified shells.'

By contrast, Moslem pilgrimage to Jerusalem greatly declined during the Ottoman period. As we have seen, while Abd el-Malik succeeded in putting the city on the Islamic map through his construction of the magnificent Dome of the Rock, Jerusalem could never equal the appeal to Moslems of Mecca or Medina (and this remains true to this day). Thus, pious Moslems continued to make the journey to Mecca, and they would visit Jerusalem only if it happened to lie along their route. Few indeed were the Moslems of other lands who would set out on a pilgrimage to Jerusalem alone. The Haram esh-Sharif, over the centuries, thus became a pilgrim centre only for those Moslems who lived within the borders of Palestine. During the Ottoman administration, however, even they stopped coming to Jerusalem. Impoverished by pernicious taxation, their houses, lands and villages in ruin or decay, those dwelling in Galilee or southern Judea, far from the city, were too preoccupied with the problem of subsistence to think of trekking to Jerusalem. In the later years of Turkish rule, the Dome of the Rock and the Mosque of El-Aksa served mainly the Moslems living in and around Jerusalem.

The reasons which brought a decline in Moslem pilgrimage also kept Moslem settlement in the country during the nineteenth century virtually static. The Christian community, too, failed to show any increase (though Christian fortunes in this period were advanced through the support given to the various sects by France, Britain, Russia and, later, Germany – who were moved as much by economic and political as by religious interests). The land remained 'almost uninhabited', as Hasselquist had observed in the previous century. The Jewish population, however, grew, and grew steeply in the latter half of the century with the resurgence of the 'Return to Zion' movement. Pilgrimage, and thrice daily prayer, had kept alive throughout nineteen centuries of exile the Jewish hope of regained freedom in their National Home. The spirit thus nurtured now fuelled the practical project to 'redeem' the neglected soil of ancient Israel and revive Jewish sovereignty, and young Jewish pioneers journeyed to Palestine (joining the Jewish remnant which had always been in the country) and set about the back-breaking work of clearing swamp and terracing the stony hillsides, thrusting back the desert and preparing the reclaimed land for cultivation. In the bleak areas of the coastal plain they founded farm villages which are cities today; and in established towns, like Jerusalem, they began settling outside the walls, an almost unheard of phenomenon at the time. One of the men who furthered this development was the most renowned Jewish pilgrim of the century, Sir Moses Montefiore of England, who made his first pilgrimage to the Holy Land in 1836 and his last in 1875, at the age of 91. He was responsible for starting the construction of a Jewish artisans quarter outside the Jerusalem city gates in 1860, and leading Jerusalem families followed with the establishment of residential suburbs to the west of the Old City. By the end of the century, Jerusalem had a Jewish majority, and added to the map of the country were new agricultural settlements.

This process, notably the reclamation of swamp and desert by Jewish pioneer settlers and their creation of new farming communities throughout the land, was greatly expanded in the years that followed, and to them goes much of the credit for laying the practical foundations of Israel's renewed statehood. The attainment of this goal was given great stimulus by the founding in 1897 of the World Zionist Organization as the organized political instrument of the Jewish yearning for independence. Twenty years later came both the Balfour Declaration (November 1917), Britain's commitment favouring 'the establishment of a national home for the Jewish people', and the entry into Jerusalem of the British military commander, General Allenby (December 1917). By September 1918, Allenby had conquered the rest of the country, and the 400-year-old Ottoman empire came to an end.

Palestine remained under British control for the next thirty years, at first under a military administration and then under a League of Nations Mandate which incorporated the Balfour Declaration. Suddenly, there was a turning of the tide. The centuries-old process of neglect, decay, erosion and devastation was arrested and reversed. No longer hampered by Ottoman restriction, and backed by the League of Nations charter, the Jews launched themselves into a revolutionary development of the country, the like of which, for tempo and sheer pioneering effort, the land had never known. With this dynamism came more Jewish immigration and settlement – and this in turn attracted immigration of Arabs from the neighbouring Moslem lands, thus reversing a process for them, too; for in the preceding centuries, Palestine had been a land from which Arabs emigrated. This development received little aid from the British Administration, for on the political level, and with the emergence of Arab hostility to the idea of a Jewish National Home, the British grew cool towards their Balfour commitment and sought the appearance of maintaining an even-handed policy towards Arab and Jew. What development projects they did undertake were designed largely for the Arab sector, since the Jews seemed able to look after themselves.

At the technical level, however, the Mandatory Government gave Palestine, for the first time in many centuries, civilized administration, introducing the rule of law and checking corruption and chaos. This, together with Jewish development and the vastly improved means of communication from the west, produced a revolutionary expansion in the volume of Jewish and Christian pilgrimage. Not since the early years of the Crusader period were Christians so free to visit their sacred shrines. Indeed, they were even more free, for there was now no fear of Saracen attack to impede their movement to Nazareth and the Sea of Galilee in the north, Jerusalem and the Judean desert in the centre, and the Sinai monastery in the south. Jewish pilgrims flocked to the country, freer than they had been in all the years of their exile to visit their holy places, and also drawn by the exciting accomplishments of the Jewish settlers. Moslem pilgrimage remained fairly static, the re-drawn map of the Middle East prompting those who could travel to favour the journey to Mecca.

Under the British Administration, there was thus freedom of access to the shrines

Tomb of the Patriarchs — the Cave of Machpelah — in Hebron, as seen from a nearby olive grove

of the three creeds, although the Moslem prohibition against Jews from entering the Haram, site of the Jewish Temple Mount, was maintained – Christians were allowed in – and the British also respected the Moslem ban on the entry of Jews into the Cave of the Hebrew Patriarchs in Hebron. The British, on the whole, maintained the religious status quo, refusing, for example, the requests of Christian leaders to restore, as one of them put it, 'churches and convents which still lay in ruins, or had been turned into mosques, dwelling houses and stables by the intolerance of Islam'. There was no wish to arouse Moslem anger by returning to the Christians and Jews the churches and synagogues which Islam had taken from them.

The British Mandate ended on 14 May 1948, and on that day the State of Israel was established. That night, Tel Aviv was bombed by the Egyptian Air Force, and next day the regular armies of all the neighbouring Arab states invaded the new-born country. Israel had to fight a grim War of Independence against outrageous odds. But she emerged victorious, driving out the Arab armies in a series of daring battles, and in the first half of 1949, Egypt, Lebanon, Transjordan and Syria signed armistice agreements with her, the armistice frontiers roughly conforming to the positions held by the rival forces.

Of relevance to the story of pilgrimage is the armistice agreement signed with Transjordan (as it was then called – now the Hashemite Kingdom of Jordan). At the close of the fighting, Jerusalem was a divided city, the western half (together with Mount Scopus and Mount Zion) in Israel, and roughly the eastern half in Jordan. This placed the Old City and the Jewish cemetery on the Mount of Olives within Jordan control, and with them the main holy places of all three religions – the Church of the Holy Sepulchre, the Haram esh-Sharif and the Western Wall. Bethlehem, with its Church of the Nativity, and the Tomb of Rachel on its outskirts, remained Jordanian, and so did Hebron, with its tombs of the Hebrew Patriarchs. The principal holy places on the itinerary of pilgrims which were within Israel territory were the Christian Coenaculum and the Jewish Tomb of David on Jerusalem's Mount Zion, the Church of the Annunciation in Nazareth, and the numerous shrines, Christian and Jewish, in Galilee, including the Mount of Beatitudes, the Capernaum synagogue and Tabgha, as well as the Jewish sites at Safad and Meron, Tiberias and other historic locations on the shores of the Sea of Galilee.

With the conclusion of this armistice agreement, it was agreed between the two States that talks would immediately follow to deal with 'free access to the holy places' in Jerusalem, and 'use of the cemetery on the Mount of Olives', but nothing ever came of this. Jerusalem remained a divided city and the Holy Land a divided country. This caused hardship to pilgrims who wished to visit the shrines in both territories. Israel was willing to allow any pilgrim or tourist, irrespective of race or creed, to enter from Jordan via one of the crossing-points – the main one was the Mandelbaum Gate in Jerusalem – through which diplomats, United

Nations personnel and clergy would pass from one side to the other. Jordan, how-ever, maintained a general ban on visitors coming from Israel, and was loth to allow them to leave Jordan by crossing into Israel. Thus, a Christian pilgrim who wished to visit those places where Jesus spent his youth and early ministry, and those associated with his last hours, would proceed to one side, then fly to Cyprus and board another plane to complete his visits on the other side. A Jewish pilgrim had to satisfy himself with the shrines in Israel alone, for he was not allowed into Jordan at all. Most grievous was the denial to Jews of access to the Western Wall.

Over the years, there was a slight Jordanian relaxation of the regulations for Christians and Moslems, Jordan allowing a few hundred Moslems in Israel to visit the Mosque of El-Aksa during Ramadan, and a similar number of Israel Christians to cross the lines at Easter and Christmas. At Easter, they would take part in the colourful processions and services held by the Latin Church, or in the exotic cere-mony of the 'Holy Fire' conducted by the Greek Orthodox in the Church of the Holy Sepulchre. At Christmas, they would join in the pomp and pageantry of the Latin patriarch's procession from Jerusalem to Bethlehem and attend the Pontifical midnight mass in the Church of St Catherine adjoining the Basilica of the Nativity. Members of the Greek Orthodox Church (who celebrate Christmas on 7 January, according to the Julian calendar) would follow their patriarch and archbishops, attired in luxurious vestments, in a similarly traditional procession to Bethlehem, but they were entitled to hold their midnight mass in the Church of the Nativity itself. (So were the Armenian Christians, who celebrate their Christ-mas a week later.) In more recent years, many organized groups of pilgrims were permitted to cross either way, and not only at festival time, through the Mandel-baum Gate.

During this period of Israel statehood, Jewish and Christian pilgrims began ar-riving in large numbers. This of course was a period when travel became a popular diversion, with rapid air services and none of the dangers and discomforts which had faced the early pilgrims. However, a major attraction for visitors of both creeds were the dramatic accomplishments of the new State; the rise of new cities and villages on ancient biblical sites – and bearing the same names – where the fore-fathers of the modern Israelis had lived and worked and battled and prophesied; the exciting discoveries in the field of biblical archaeology by the numerous scien-tific expeditions; and the extraordinary restoration programme of ancient sites. All this gave a new dimension to pilgrimage. The Bible came alive.

The Jewish pilgrim, in particular, found much to satisfy him in Israel; for though bereft of its holiest shrine, Israel still held most of the historic places associated with the history of his people. Moreover, he could also celebrate the three Pilgrim Festivals in a unique manner. The whole of Israel at festival time wears a special dress and mood; all work ceases; and the synagogues are thronged.

At Passover, the great Jewish festival of freedom, all participate in the ritual meal

The carriage in which Sir Moses Montefiore made his ninetenth century pilgrimages to the Holy Land
Overleaf: The Sea of Galilee, with the hill-top city of Safad in the distance (top right)

called the Seder, at which they read the Haggada, the story of the exodus from Egypt and the liberation of the Children of Israel from bondage, and partake of certain foods symbolic of the dramatic events of that liberation. They eat matza, unleavened bread, to remind them of the haste with which their forbears departed (so that there was no time for the dough to rise). They taste bitter herbs to recall the harsh life and labour suffered by the Israelite slaves. And they place a shank bone on the table to represent the paschal lamb whose blood was sprinkled on the Israelite dwellings as a guide to the angel of death to 'pass over' them on his way to afflict the Egyptians. Four goblets of ritual wine are drunk during the recital. In Israel, this is an occasion when every Jew, citizen and pilgrim, feels a personal identification with these happenings in his people's past, as if he himself were an Israelite launching himself into freedom and eventually reaching the Promised Land.

Succot, the Feast of Tabernacles, recalls the improvised booths which the Children of Israel used in their wanderings through the wilderness, and today, in town and village throughout Israel, the holiday is marked by the erection of booths (succot in Hebrew) in the courts or balconies of the houses. The celebration, indeed, is exactly reminiscent of the days of Ezra and Nehemiah, when the people were enjoined to 'go forth unto the mount, and fetch olive branches, and pine branches, and myrtle branches, and palm branches, and branches of thick trees, to make booths as it is written. So the people went forth, and brought them, and made themselves booths, every one upon the roof of his house, and in their courts, and in the courts of the house of God, and in the street of the water gate...' The annual sight in the Jewish State of today during the preparatory days of the Pilgrim Festival of Succot is also of people bearing 'pine branches' and 'palm branches' and 'myrtle leaves' through the streets to their homes, and, in the markets, selecting an unblemished citron (etrog) and finely formed palm (lulav) for the ritual procession in the synagogue. In Israel the booths are decorated with lamps and flowers and clusters of new fruits, and those of the oriental communities are hung with rich tapestries and exotic carpets from Bukhara and Persia.

The Feast of Weeks (Shavuot) marks both the giving of the Law to Moses on Mount Sinai and also the gathering-in of the first fruits. Synagogues are decked with flowers and the portions of the Torah selected for recital are those of the Ten Commandments and the injunctions covering harvest offerings. But Israel is now able to celebrate the agricultural part of the festival in a manner denied to them during the centuries of exile; for the Jews are now cultivating their ancient soil and can mark the beginning of the harvest in the time-honoured manner. In rural settlements throughout the country, farm waggons and floats, colourfully adorned and bearing the newly harvested produce in decorative display, move by in festive procession, flanked by boys and girls singing psalms and harvest songs. The procession ends with traditional folk dance in which all participate, moving to the rhythm of appropriate biblical verses set to music.

Seder service on the Pilgrim Festival of Passover being celebrated in traditional style at the home in Jerusalem of a Bukharan Jewish family

The most memorable celebration of Shavuot in our (and possibly in any) generation took place on Wednesday, 14 June 1967, exactly one week after Jerusalem was re-united on the third day of the Six Day War. The city still bore signs of the grim fighting as a quarter of a million Jews from all parts of the country, including soldiers who had helped to liberate it, moved through the nearby Dung Gate in the southern wall, past notices marked 'Danger: Mines', and converged on the Western Wall in a mass pilgrimage. It was the largest, and probably the most moving, pilgrimage to the relic of the Second Temple since the great exile and dispersion nineteen centuries earlier.

The Six Day War changed the pattern of pilgrimage for members of all three faiths. Not only Jerusalem but the entire Holy Land had again become one under Israel authority, and at the end of the fighting the Government of Israel announced that persons of all three religions, Christians, Moslems and Jews, would have free access to their holy places on either side of the former divisive frontier. Since June 1967, for the first time ever, this freedom is absolute, and each faith is responsible for its own holy places. There is no Saracen guard to control Christian entry into the Church of the Holy Sepulchre; no Crusader to bar the Moslem from the Haram esh-Sharif; and neither Christian nor Moslem to prevent the Jewish pilgrim from visiting the Temple Mount, sounding the Shofar at the Western Wall, or entering the Cave of Machpelah in Hebron. Moslem and Christian Arabs living east or west of the old frontier can now pray together at their holy shrines, and not only at Ramadan or Easter or Christmas but any day of the year. Overseas pilgrims have no more 'no man's land' to cross and no further need to fly in and out of Cyprus to reach all the pilgrimage sites.

With the barriers down since 1967, small wonder that the number of pilgrims of all faiths has risen to an average approaching half a million a year. It is a sobering thought that, at the very period when the Middle East is beset by turmoil and conflict, Israel, which lies in its midst, should exercise so powerful an appeal to pilgrims that they stream into the country on a scale never before known in its history. Today more than ever, the Land of the Bible is indeed the Land of Pilgrimage.

INDEX

(numbers in bold type indicate illustrations)

ACKNOWLEDGEMENTS

The authors and publishers are indebted to the following institutions for help in providing illustrations:
Aldus 138; Alinari 32; Armenian Patriarchate, Jerusalem 120, 182; Bibliothèque Nationale, Paris 49; Bob Jones University Gallery, Greenville, S.C. 14; British Museum 131; Custodia della Terra Sancta 83, 114, 151, 155, 166, 176; Ecole Biblique et Archaeologique Française, Jerusalem 92; Escorial 127; Greek-Orthodox Patriarchate 91 top left, 123; Holyland Hotel, Jerusalem 28; Israel Department of Antiquities 40, 62–3, 91 bottom left, 95, 98, 134, 146–7, 149; Israel Exploration Society 41; Israel Museum, Jerusalem 13, 25, 53, 105, 145; Jewish National and University Library 3, 87, 186–7; Teddy Kollek Collection endpapers, 117, 174; Landesbibliothek, Gotha 56, 164–5; Maritime Museum, Haifa 88; Studium Biblicum Franciscanum (Convent of the Flagellation), Jerusalem 39, 138 above; Walters Art Gallery, Baltimore 55

The photographers whose works appear in this books are as follows:
Alinari 44–5; Ben-Dov 117 below; Bonfils 176; Werner Braun 4, 22, 25 top, 26–7, 84, 141, 150, 170, 185, 195; Hillel Burger 40; Boris Carmi 119, 142; Richard Cleave 17, 57; Fred Csaznik 137; Amiram Erev 43, 101–2, 156, 163; George Gerster 69; David Harris 3, 25 below, 28, 39, 46, 64, 72–5, 87, 91 top left, bottom left, 105, 115, 117 top, 120, 132–3, 138 top, 145, 152, 174, 186–7, 188–9, 199, 202; Hal Larson 173; Reuven Milon 21, 110; Garo Nalbandijan 35, 71, 79, 123, 179; Zeev Radovan 13 top, 31, 76, 91 right, 182; Chanan Sadeh 88; Ronald Sheridan 128, 148, 180–1, 200–1; Alex Strajmayster 61, 70, 96–7, 109, 113